WHY *did this* HAPPEN? WHAT *is GOD* DOING?

WHY
did this
HAPPEN?
WHAT
is GOD
DOING?

Diane Kannady

TruConnections
PRESS

Published by TruConnections Press

ISBN 13: 978-0-9846967-2-7

DEDICATION

This book is dedicated to the Riches in Christ family. Without your love, friendship, prayers and support, this book would not have been possible. Thank you.

May our hunger to know God more fully and to represent Him more accurately be ever increasing.

CONTENTS

INTRODUCTION

When troubles come our way, two questions naturally arise: *Why did this happen? What is God doing?* If we can't accurately answer these questions, our hard times will be even harder. Incorrect answers produce confusion and added emotional pain on top of the difficulties themselves.

- People become angry and bitter at God for allowing the hardships they face and they struggle with how a loving God could permit such a thing.

- Individuals fret over whether God is testing or teaching them as they frantically try to discern what message the Lord is sending through their ordeal.

- Others wonder if their circumstance is punishment from God and agonize over what they may have done to deserve such tribulation.

However, according to the Bible, adversity does not come from God. It's part of life in a fallen world. Although God does not instigate life's challenges, He does use them for good and cause them to serve His purposes.

In this book, we will examine what the Bible says about why bad things happen and what God does in the midst of hard times so that we can rightly answer these important questions. Accurate answers will help us deal with the struggles of life in a way that honors God and brings us victory.

PART ONE:

ANSWERING THE *WHY* AND *WHAT* QUESTIONS

THE *WHY* QUESTION

Why did this happen? is probably the first question people ask in the face of unexpected adversity. Although *why* is a natural reaction, it isn't the best question to ask because it will undermine our trust in God. Whether we realize it or not, when we ask *why*, we imply that God has been unfair in allowing our trouble.

We must learn to shut the door on this thought. Such thinking erodes our confidence in the Lord at the very time we need to turn to Him for help. If we believe that God is behind our misfortune in any way, how can we be certain of His help as we deal with the situation?

Satan is ultimately behind all accusations against God as he seeks to weaken our reliance on our Heavenly Father. That's what he did to Adam and Eve. He brought a charge against the Lord to entice them to disobey God. Satan told Eve that God ordered her and Adam to refrain from eating the fruit of the tree of the knowledge of good and evil because He was withholding something from them.

" 'You won't die (if you eat)*' the serpent hissed. 'God knows that your eyes will be opened when you eat it. You will become just like God, knowing everything, both good and evil '"* (Genesis 3:4-5, NLT).

Satan uses the same strategy on people today. He challenges God's goodness by claiming that the Lord is behind the hardships and sufferings of this life. But God is never the source or the cause of your woes.

In the face of adversity, it isn't wrong to ask: *Why did this happen?* However, you must be able to rightly answer that question according to the scripture. Otherwise, you are vulnerable to the maneuvers of the devil.

Why do bad things happen? Tragic, tormenting, destructive, difficult circumstances are part of life in an earth that has been damaged by sin. This is the correct answer to the *why* question.

A CURSE IN THE EARTH

As we study the Bible, we find that death and corruption entered creation through the sin of the first man. God commanded Adam not to eat the fruit of the forbidden tree and he violated that command. Adam's decision had significant consequences for mankind and the earth.

"When Adam sinned, sin entered the entire human race. His sin spread death throughout all the world, so that everything began to grow old and die" (Romans 5:12, TLB).

2

> "(God said) *Cursed is the ground because of you*
> (Adam)*; In toil you will eat of it all the days of your*
> *life"* (Genesis 3:17, NASB). *"It will grow thorns and*
> *thistles for you, and you shall eat its grasses. All your*
> *life you will sweat to master it, until your dying day.*
> *Then you will return to the ground from which you*
> *came"* (Genesis 3:18-19, TLB).

Adam's sin caused the curse of death to enter the earth and the material world became subject to decay. That means if you leave a peach sitting on the kitchen counter, it will eventually rot. Not because God made peaches to rot, but due to the effects of that first sin. Adam and Eve's sin corrupted the natural laws and processes set into motion by God at the beginning of time. This change resulted in blight, drought, famine, destructive storms and earthquakes throughout the world.

The effects of Adam's disobedience also touched the human race and produced a sin nature in men (Romans 5:19). The results quickly became apparent. Adam and Eve's firstborn son, Cain, murdered their second son, Abel, and then lied to God about it. This inclination toward evil continued to express itself in each subsequent generation.

Additionally, when Adam gave into temptation, he gave up his God-given authority over the earth to Satan and altered the earth's power structure. The devil became the god of this world (Genesis 1:26-28; Luke 4:6; 2 Corinthians 4:4). Since then, he has roamed the earth seeking to destroy men and women by enticing them to follow him in rebellion against God (1 Peter 5:8; Ephesians 6:11-12).

As a result of Adam's sin, all human beings are born into a fallen world. This means all of us must deal daily with the

WHY DID THIS HAPPEN? WHAT IS GOD DOING?

changes produced in creation by our first parent's sin. Weeds, decay, natural disasters and death are currently part of the earth's makeup. We have bodies that are mortal and subject to sickness, old age and death. We interact with people who make unwise and sinful choices that can directly affect our lives in negative ways. Each of these factors makes life on this planet toilsome.

IS IT GOD OR THE DEVIL?

Many people have the idea that everything that happens has a direct and immediate cause. Either God did it or the devil did it. However, difficult circumstances are not the work of God or even, necessarily, the devil. They are simply part of life in a sin cursed earth.

God does not orchestrate the troubles and trials of life. We know this from what Jesus shows us about God. As we read through the New Testament accounts of Jesus' time on earth (the Gospels), we find that He did not set up circumstances to test people nor did He send trials and storms to teach or strengthen individuals. He didn't cause donkey cart crashes to discipline men. He made no one sick nor did He refuse to heal anyone who came to Him for help. If Jesus doesn't cause troubles, then we know God the Father doesn't either because Jesus does only what He sees the Father do.

> "(Jesus said) *I tell you the truth, the Son can do nothing by himself; he can do only what he sees his Father doing, because whatever the Father does the Son also does. For the Father loves the Son and shows him all he does"* (John 5:19-20, NIV).

When Jesus' disciples asked Him to show them the Father, He replied: *"Anyone who has seen me has seen the Father"* (John 14:9, NIV). Jesus showed them the Father by speaking the words and doing the works of the Father by His Father's power resident in Him. (For a complete discussion of the issues raised by these statements, read my book *God is Good and Good Means Good.*)

The devil isn't directly responsible for every tragedy either. Certainly, as the first rebel in the universe who lured Adam and Eve into sin, the devil is ultimately behind the hell and heartache in this world. But he does not instigate every adverse event in our lives. Nowhere does the Bible tell Christians to beware of the power of the devil. Rather, it instructs us to be on guard against his mental strategies as he seeks to influence human behavior. The devil works through the fallen natures of men who are not surrendered to God and he lies to the minds of those unaware of his tactics.

"(Satan) is the spirit at work in the hearts of those who refuse to obey God" (Ephesians 2:2, NLT).

"But I am afraid that your minds will be led away from your true and pure following of Christ just as Eve was tricked by the snake (Satan) *with his evil ways"* (2 Corinthians 11:3, NCV).

"Put on the full armor of God, so that you will be able to stand firm against the schemes of the devil" (Ephesians 6:11, NASB).

SOME THINGS JUST HAPPEN

We must understand that a lot of things *just happen*. We mentioned earlier that Adam's disobedience affected natural laws and processes instituted by God at creation. Even though these laws have been altered by the curse of sin, they still function and sometimes result in calamity and destruction. For example:

- God created gravity to bless mankind. But the law of gravity often leads to injury or death when people with mortal bodies violate that law through ignorance or carelessness. God didn't do it. The devil didn't do it. It happened because that's life in a sin cursed earth.

- God created trees to bless mankind. But large trees occasionally blow over during violent storms and crush cars and houses. Why? Because destructive storms (products of corrupted natural processes) blow over trees weakened by disease and aging (also products of the curse of death in creation). God didn't do it. The devil didn't do it. It's simply life in a fallen world.

You hear people say: "There are no coincidences in life. Everything happens for a reason." These statements may be common, but they aren't true. According to Jesus, some things *do* happen by chance. He made that clear as He talked about a man who was attacked by robbers while he traveled on a dangerous road. Two religious leaders passed the wounded man and left him, but a Good Samaritan stopped to help. Note one point Jesus made when he described what occurred.

6

*"A certain man went down from Jerusalem to Jericho, and fell among thieves, which stripped him of his raiment, and wounded him, and departed, leaving him half dead. And **by chance** there came down a certain priest that way: and when he saw him, he passed by on the other side"* (Luke 10:30-31).

Notice, Jesus said the priest's presence there that day was *by chance.* The New Testament was originally written in Greek. The word translated chance means "accident" or "coincidence." *"Now **by coincidence** a certain priest was going down along that road"* (AMP). According to *Webster's Dictionary*, coincidence refers to two things that happen at the same time by accident, unintentionally or unexpectedly. Chance has to do with the way things take place. It indicates possibility.

If you toss a coin into the air, there is a chance that it will land on its head or its tail. Why are there two different possible outcomes? A number of factors can vary and affect the final result, including how hard the coin is thrown, the speed of the coin as it rises and falls, and the wind velocity at the moment of the toss. If any of these elements change even slightly, they will affect the end result.

In the story Jesus told, there were several factors that could have changed how the incident unfolded. Had any of the people involved traveled on another day, the outcome would have been altered. If the robbers had chosen a different road on which to ambush people, there would have been no crime there that day. If the injured man had fallen into a ditch not visible from the road, the Good Samaritan may not have seen the victim. If the priest or the Samaritan had another attitude about helping people, this drama would have ended differently. That is chance.

Many variable factors affect events at any given moment—choices, timing, attitudes and environmental conditions, to name a few. Therefore, lots of things in this life happen by chance. Many happenings are random. Random means "haphazard" or "determined by accident rather than design or plan." If I run over a nail and it wrecks my tire, that's an accident or a random occurrence. I didn't plan or expect the tire damage. It happened because certain factors came together by chance—my choice to drive down that street, the presence and location of the nail in the road, and the position of the tire as I approached the nail. In this life, many things *just happen*—randomly, accidently or by chance—because that's the way life is in a sin cursed world.

Before we go any further, we need to address some issues that could arise based on what we've covered so far. You may wonder how random events can occur when a sovereign God reigns over this universe. The presence of random events in no way diminishes God's sovereignty. The fact that God is sovereign means He is all powerful and the highest authority. Because God is sovereign, He is able to use the chance happenings of life in a world damaged by sin and cause them to serve His purposes. We'll discuss this more fully in a moment.

You also may be concerned that what I've said up to this point means that there is no protection against the randomness and chance of life. I'll say some things later in the book that give insight into this issue. For the moment, consider these thoughts:

- There is no such thing as a trouble-free life in this world's present state. We all face problems and trials. But God's guidance, provision and protection are available to us as we navigate through the difficulties of life.

- Jesus Himself said, *"In the world you have tribulation and trials and distress and frustration; but be of good cheer—take courage, be confident, certain, undaunted—for I have overcome the world. —I have deprived it of power to harm, have conquered it [for you]"* (John 16:33, AMP).

YES, BUT GOD ALLOWED IT

Misuse of the phrase *God allowed it* further complicates our understanding of the source of the hardships and pain in this world. We would do well to drop this phrase from our vocabulary because of the inaccurate implications attached to it. When something bad happens, people often say that although God may not have *caused* the event, He did *allow* it. Implicit in that statement is the idea that God is behind or approving of a negative circumstance because He didn't prevent it from occurring. However, there are many things that God doesn't stop, not because He approves of them, but because of the way the world is set up.

God gave men free will when He created mankind, which opened the possibility of willful disobedience against God. In this world, people regularly sin and commit horrific acts of immorality and violence. Although God is not for or behind this disobedience in any way, He doesn't interfere because men and women have the freedom to choose.

In addition to initial choices, free will also brings the consequences of those choices. Many things happen due to the sinful activities of men—occurrences that displease God and are contrary to His will. But if God wiped out or lessened the consequences of the willful actions of men and women, then humanity would not truly have free will.

Adam, the first man to receive free will, chose to sin. As we discussed earlier in the chapter, his disobedience produced cataclysmic results in the earth—results we still deal with today. When a catastrophic storm ravages a town, it's not because *God allowed it*. Such destruction is the fruit of Adam's free will choice.

As the greatest power in the universe, God could potentially stop every sin and every effect of sin, including Adam's. However, He has elected to limit Himself to human choice and the ensuing consequences. In a later chapter, I'll discuss how the Lord uses choice and consequences, including those contrary to His will.

GOD HAS A PURPOSE

God has a purpose is another misused phrase uttered by people when affliction comes their way. These words suggest that their trouble is somehow God's will for them. This idea is incorrect because it is contrary to what Jesus shows us about God. Jesus only did what He saw His Father do and He clearly contrasted His works with destructive, harmful events: *"A thief comes to steal and kill and destroy, but I* (Jesus) *came to give life—life in all its fullness"* (John 10:10, NCV). His statement makes it clear that if something kills, steals or destroys, it's not from Jesus or His Father.

Since calamity doesn't come from God, then He *cannot* have a purpose in it. Yet, just because God doesn't have a purpose in painful circumstances doesn't mean He has *no purpose*. According to *Webster's Dictionary*, a purpose is "something set up as an end to be attained." The Bible tells us that God has had a plan and a purpose since before He formed the earth.

10

Romans 8:28 speaks of those *"who have been called according to his* (God's) *purpose"* (NIV). The passage goes on to state that purpose: *"For God, in his foreknowledge, chose* (us) *to bear the family likeness of his Son, that he might be the eldest of a family of many brothers"* (Romans 8:29, J.B. Phillips). God's intention, since before creation, was and is to have a family. We are called to become sons and daughters of God.

When Jesus took on flesh in the womb of the Virgin Mary, He became fully man without ceasing to be fully God. During His years on earth, Jesus put aside His rights and privileges as God and lived as a man in dependence on God the Father. In doing so, He showed us what sons of God look like and how they act.

Jesus then went to the Cross and died in our place for our sins. His death and resurrection made it possible for us to become God's children when we put faith in Him and His sacrifice. Romans 8:30 describes the process by which God accomplishes His plan to have offspring who resemble Jesus.

"And those whom He thus foreordained He also called; and those whom He called He also justified— acquitted, made righteous, putting them into right standing with Himself. And those whom He justified He also glorified—raising them to a heavenly dignity and condition [state of being]" (Romans 8:30, AMP).

We cannot give a detailed explanation in this short book of how God fashions men into the likeness of Jesus by justifying and glorifying them. Suffice it to say that God accomplishes His plan through the Cross, which paid man's debt for sin and opened the way for His Spirit to work in men and transform

11

them. God does not have a hidden purpose in a car wreck or an illness. His purpose, since before time began, has been to make sinful men into sons like Jesus through the process of salvation.

In our effort to find meaning in and make sense of happenings we do not understand, we often look for God's purpose in specific situations. But God's aim is bigger than singular events. His eternal plan is to have a family of sons and daughters who are like Jesus in character, power, holiness and love. God wants a family obtained through the power of the Cross.

We only quoted part of Romans 8:28 earlier. The entire verse says: *"And we know that God causes all things to work together for good to those who love God, to those who are called according to His purpose"* (NASB). This passage assures us that God is able to cause everything that happens—including things He has no purpose in—to serve His purpose of gathering a family. Because He is sovereign, God can take random events and sinful choices and use them to further His plan to have sons and daughters. And as He does, He brings great good out of real evil. I'll explain this concept in more detail in upcoming chapters.

› ⟶⟩⟩⟩▸ · ◂⟨⟨⟨⟵ ‹

You might be thinking: "Even if God is not the source of our trials, why doesn't He intervene more in the calamities of life? After all, He is not only powerful, He is loving and compassionate." The next few chapters will provide more insight as we continue to answer the *why* question.

SUFFERING AND THE BIG PICTURE

*W*hen people ask *why*, they usually are asking in reference to a specific situation. "Why did this happen to me?" "Why did that happen to them?" If you try to understand human suffering and pain by starting with your particular situation or someone else's, you may draw wrong conclusions about God and how He works. You have to start with the big picture and understand your circumstances in terms of God's overall plan.

THE BIG PICTURE

In eternity past, God designed a plan to have a family. He made the earth to be a home for Himself and His family. Then He created human beings with the intention that they become His sons and daughters. That's the big picture.

> *"Long ago, even before he made the world, God loved us and chose us in Christ to be holy and without fault in his eyes. His unchanging plan has always been to adopt us into his own family by bringing us to himself through Jesus Christ. And this gave him great pleasure"* (Ephesians 1:4-5, NLT).

"He made the world to be lived in, not to be a place of empty chaos" (Isaiah 45:18, NLT).

"I heard a loud shout from the throne, saying, 'Look, the home of God is now among his people! He will live with them, and they will be his people. God himself will be with them'" (Revelation 21:3, NLT).

"And I will be their God, and they will be my children" (Revelation 21:7, NLT).

As we have already discussed, the world and the human race were damaged by sin after their creation. However, God was not taken by surprise. He created mankind knowing that they would choose independence from Him through disobedience. As part of His eternal plan, God devised a way to deal with this rebellion and the subsequent curse of death in the earth. God Himself took on flesh, came to earth and died for the sins of men. Revelation 13:8 refers to Jesus as *"the Lamb that was slain [in sacrifice] from the foundation of the world"* (AMP).

At the Cross, Jesus took our sin on Himself to remove it and undo the damage done by it. Consequently, all who bow their knee to the Lord Jesus Christ and accept His sacrifice for their sins are restored to God's original purpose. They become His sons and daughters.

GOD'S PRESENT PURPOSE

God's main goal right now is not to make life easy and painless for everyone. His primary purpose is to bring all men to salvation from sin and to make them His children through faith in Christ. God is much more concerned about the eternal destiny of men than He is with stopping every instance of suffering and injustice in this life. If a person has a perfect, pain-free life now but ends up eternally separated from God because of his sin, this wonderful life is all for naught.

Consider something Jesus said as He was teaching one day. Someone called to Him from the crowd and asked Jesus to order his brother to divide their father's estate with him. The Lord answered: *"Beware! Don't be greedy for what you don't have. Real life is not measured by how much we own"* (Luke 12:15, NLT).

He then related a parable about a rich man who owned a very successful farm that produced such abundant crops that his barns overflowed. The man decided to tear down the existing barns and build bigger ones.

> *"And I'll sit back and say to myself, My friend, you have enough stored away for years to come. Now take it easy! Eat, drink, and be merry! But God said to him, 'You fool! You will die this very night. Then who will get it all?' Yes, a person is a fool to store up earthly wealth but not have a rich relationship with God"* (Luke 12:19-21, NLT).

Although Jesus was specifically addressing greediness in His answer, we can learn something important for our discussion. According to Jesus, if you have a wonderful, problem-free life with all the best things this world can offer yet have no relationship with God through faith in Christ, life means nothing.

Because of the nature of life in a sin cursed earth, individuals experience heartache and loss and many needs and desires go unmet. Even if you live a life of success and

15

abundance and achieve all your dreams, old age and death take it away. That doesn't mean there is no provision for help, happiness, supply and protection in this life. There is. But life on earth will not be pain-free or problem-free until every trace of sin and its effects are removed at the Second Coming of Jesus.

The last two chapters of the Book of Revelation speak of the changes that will occur when Jesus returns to earth. They give us a tantalizing hint of the life that is ahead.

> *"God will wipe away every tear from* (our) *eyes, and death shall be no more, neither shall there be anguish—sorrow and mourning—nor grief nor pain any more; for the old conditions and the former order of things have passed away"* (Revelation 21:4, AMP).

> *"And there shall be no more curse"* (Revelation 22:3).

AN ETERNAL PERSPECTIVE

We must also realize that life on this earth in its present condition—groaning under the weight of sin and the curse of death—is only a tiny part of God's plan for us. We are eternal beings. The greater portion of our existence is after this life, first in Heaven and then on the new earth. The new earth will be the old earth transformed and freed from the curse of sin and death (Isaiah 65:17; 2 Peter 3:13).

The life to come won't just be the removal of troubles and pain. It will provide compensation. All will be made right. God won't merely wipe away tears. He'll replace them with joy. The sufferings of this life don't compare with what is ahead. Six to ten thousand years of human history on this fallen earth and all the suffering endured by men is small in comparison to eternity and what awaits us.

"Whatever we may have to go through now is less than nothing compared with the magnificent future God has in store for us. The whole creation is on tiptoe to see the wonderful sight of the sons of God coming into their own" (Romans 8:18-19, J.B. Phillips).

"For all creation is waiting patiently and hopefully for that future day when God will resurrect his children. For on that day thorns and thistles, sin, death, and decay—the things that overcame the world against its will at God's command—will all disappear, and the world around us will share in the glorious freedom from sin which God's children enjoy" (Romans 8:19-21, TLB).

I am in no way minimizing the pain people experience in this life. However, a proper perspective on the big picture can lighten the load of our hardships. When a child loses a favorite toy or when a teenager doesn't get a date to the dance, their hearts truly are broken. But from the standpoint of adulthood and in terms of an entire life span, we realize these issues are not as devastating as they seem in the moment.

I'm also not suggesting that the anguish of losing a loved one equals the loss of a toy or that the molestation of an innocent boy or girl is comparable to not having a date. I am illustrating how a different perspective can lessen the weight of life's traumas. No one in Heaven is lamenting the fact that he lived in dire straits during his lifetime or that she left earth under brutal or catastrophic circumstances.

17

The losses and miseries of this present life are temporary for those who know the Lord. The ultimate stage for the reversals of this world's injustices, heartbreaks and tragedies awaits us in the life to come. This knowledge can help us make it through the many challenges we face.

GOD IS SOVEREIGN

Although we cannot avoid life's hardships, we can be encouraged by the fact that God is sovereign. Many people take God's sovereignty to mean that He is behind everything that happens, either directly or indirectly. They believe that because God is sovereign, He can do bad as well as good to people. But this view of sovereignty is contrary to what Jesus shows us about God. An accurate view of God's sovereignty recognizes that He is the supreme power and authority in the universe.

Because of His power and authority, God is able to cause everything that happens to serve His plan to have a family. He can take random acts that did not originate with Him—chance events that occur because of the chaos in this world due to sin—and cause them to serve His purposes. God can bring great good out of genuine evil as He gathers His family.

In the context of God obtaining His family, the Bible says He *"works out everything in conformity with the purpose of his will"* (Ephesians 1:11, NIV) and *"causes everything to work together for the good of those who love God and are called according to his purpose for them"* (Romans 8:28, NLT). This is welcome news for people living in a sin cursed earth where tribulation and trials are part of everyday life. In later chapters, we'll consider some spectacular examples of how God, in His sovereignty, does this. (For a more detailed discussion of

God's sovereignty, read Pages 22-32 in *God is Good and Good Means Good*.)

THE MYSTERY OF SUFFERING

Much mystery surrounds the topic of human suffering. Right now, no one can fully explain why every instance of suffering and anguish occurs. But we can't let what we don't yet understand undermine what we clearly know about the goodness of God as seen in and through Jesus.

> *"The secret things belong unto the Lord our God: but those things which are revealed belong unto us and to our children for ever"* (Deuteronomy 29:29).

If we were to cite this entire passage in Deuteronomy, we would see that the context is suffering due to sin. God warned Israel through His prophet Moses that if they abandoned Him to worship false gods—which they did—they would experience great hardship at the hands of their enemies. Even though God told them what would happen and why, He knew some would still have questions when it happened. So God admonished them ahead of time: Don't let what you *don't* understand about your situation undermine what you *do* know. We, too, should heed God's instruction.

WHY OR WHAT?

Once while reading through the Bible, I noted every instance where someone asked *why*. I discovered that few people got the answer they wanted because the Bible does not always address *why*. Rather, it directs us on what to do.

Why may be a reasonable question, but it isn't always the most important question you need answered in the midst of life's challenges. Knowing why something happened doesn't automatically solve the problem. For example, even if you know why your car won't start, you still aren't going anywhere unless you know what to do about it. Notice how Jesus answered when his disciples asked Him why a particular man was born blind.

> *"And as Jesus passed by, he saw a man which was blind from his birth. And his disciples asked him, saying, Master, who did sin, this man, or his parents, that he was born blind? Jesus answered, Neither hath this man sinned, nor his parents: but that the works of God should be made manifest in him. I must work the works of him that sent me, while it is day: the night cometh, when no man can work"* (John 9:1-4).

> *"Having said this, he spit on the ground, made some mud with the saliva, and put it on the man's eyes. 'Go,' he told him, 'Wash in the pool of Siloam.' So the man went and washed, and came home seeing"* (John 9:6-8, NIV).

Jesus did not answer the *why* question posed by His disciples that day other than to say that the man's blindness was not the result of his parents' sin or the sin of the man himself. Instead, Jesus told His disciples *what He was going to do—* work the works of God by healing the sightless man.

Before continuing, we need to briefly address a common misinterpretation of this portion of scripture. Some say that Jesus' answer meant this gentleman was born blind in accordance with God's will. They claim that God permitted the blindness so He could demonstrate His power by healing the man. This interpretation is not accurate. Consider several points:

- If the blindness was God's work, then when Jesus healed the man, He *destroyed* the work of God by *doing* the work of God. The healing and the blindness cannot both be the work of God. If this man's blindness was in agreement with God's will at any time, for any reason, then Jesus undid God's will by healing the man.

- God does not act against Himself by afflicting men only to turn around and set them free. On one occasion, the Pharisees accused Jesus of casting out devils by the power of the devil. Jesus answered them *"And if Satan cast out Satan, he is divided against himself; how shall then his kingdom stand?"* (Matthew 12:26). If the devil doesn't work against his own interests, then surely God does not. God's kingdom is not divided.

- There are more than enough sick people to go around in this fallen world. God does not need to afflict, or allow individuals to be afflicted, to provide an opportunity for Him to heal.

When we understand certain aspects of the original Greek language, it's clear that God was not behind the man's blindness in any way and that Jesus' focus was on *what to do* rather than *why*.

"And his disciples asked him, saying, Master, who did sin, this man, or his parents, that he was born blind? Jesus answered, Neither hath this man sinned, nor his

21

parents: but that the works of God should be made manifest in him. I must work the works of him that sent me, while it is day" (John 9:2-4).

Note the word *that* in both the disciples' question and Jesus' answer. In the original language, *that* is sometimes used to express purpose (why) and sometimes to express result (what). In this passage, *that* conveys result.

The disciples asked: Whose sin had *resulted* in the man's blindness? Jesus answered: Neither sin produced this blindness, but it will *result* in the man being healed. Then He directed their attention to *"What we should do."* Jesus said: I must work the works of God and heal this man.

⋅ →➤➤▸ ⋅ ◂◄◄← ⋅

Although we don't always know why specific troubles come (beyond that's life in a sin cursed earth), we do know God's goodness and His purpose. Therefore, we can be certain that He will bring good out of our troubles and cause them to serve His eternal plan to have a family. We can be assured that any loss connected with the event is temporary. And we can be confident that the heartbreak and injustice of the circumstance will one day be reversed. We'll look a little later at examples of how God does this.

GOD'S LOVE AND OUR CIRCUMSTANCES

As a Bible teacher, I've had people ask: "Why did this tragedy happen to me?" Before I can respond, they sometimes answer their own question this way: "God must not love me." Many have the idea that the good and bad events of life are expressions of God's greater or lesser love. If all is well, they are assured that God loves them. If things go wrong, they presume that God loves them less or not at all. However, the ups and downs of life are not indicators of God's love. In this chapter, we will explore the relationship between God's love and our troubles as we seek to answer the *why* question.

UNCONDITIONAL LOVE

God's love for man is unconditional, which means there is no condition we must meet to have His love and there is nothing we can do that will cost us His love. Perhaps the best way to understand this is to think of a sweet-smelling flower. It exudes a fragrance to everyone. Whether a good or bad person approaches the flower, both individuals experience the same aroma. The flower can't withhold its scent from one person and give it to the other because its nature is to be fragrant. It is the same with God's love.

God's love is not a response to something in us. He does not love you because you are good. He doesn't withhold His love from you because you are bad. God loves you because He *is* love. His love for you is an expression of something in His makeup. You have God's love, not because you did something right, but because He is love (1 John 4:8). His nature is to love. He can do nothing else.

The Lord does not hold back His love because there are flaws in you. He loves you with your flaws. In saying this, I'm not implying that it does not matter what we do. We are called to live holy lives. But the purpose of godly living is not to earn God's love and blessing. It can't be earned. Holy living glorifies God. We were created to become sons and daughters of God and to glorify Him by accurately reflecting His holiness to the world around us.

> "So that we who first hoped in Christ—who first put our confidence in Him—[have been destined and appointed] to live for the praise of His glory" (Ephesians 1:12, AMP).

> "Obey God because you are his children. Don't slip back into your old ways of doing evil; you didn't know any better then. But now you must be holy in everything you do, just as God—who chose you to be his children—is holy. For he himself has said, 'You must be holy because I am holy'" (1 Peter 1:14-16, NLT).

THE CROSS AND GOD'S LOVE

The Cross of Jesus Christ is the supreme demonstration of God's unconditional love for man. It was inspired by God's love, not by our goodness or deservingness. Through the Cross, God expressed His love for us when we were at our worst. Jesus died for you and me while we were sinners and enemies of God in full rebellion against Him.

> *"But God demonstrates his own love for us in this: While we were still sinners, Christ died for us...when we were God's enemies, we were reconciled to him through the death of his Son"* (Romans 5:8-10, NIV).

> *"This is how God showed his love among us: He sent his one and only Son into the world that we might live through him. This is love: not that we loved God, but that he loved us and sent his Son as an atoning sacrifice for our sins"* (1 John 4:9-10, NIV).

> *"For God so loved the world, that he gave his only begotten Son, that whosoever believeth in him should not perish, but have everlasting life"* (John 3:16).

God's love motivated Him to meet your greatest need—salvation from your sins. If God loved you on your worst day, which was any day before you bowed your knee to the Lord Jesus Christ, then why would He love you less now that you are His son or daughter? Why would His love for you suddenly become conditional? Why would it now be necessary to earn God's love through your actions?

The Cross of Christ is the objective standard by which we know that God loves us. When we don't feel loved by

God, the Cross triumphs over our emotions. When our mind questions how God could love someone who fails as often as we do, the Cross answers those thoughts. When the hardships of life seem to cry out that God doesn't care about us, the Cross prevails over our circumstances. The Cross shows us the regard God has for us. With this knowledge, we can silence all those seeming challenges to the certainty of God's love.

VALUE AND WORTH

Many of us find it hard to believe that God loves us because we connect value and worth with achievement, accomplishments and talents. Therefore, when we fall short or fail to measure up, we are certain that God's love for us has waned.

True value and worth, however, come from what a person is willing to pay for something. Consider this example: A lady has a garage sale and one of the items she sets out is a lamp. She never liked it. It was given to her by someone she doesn't care for. From her perspective, the lamp is a piece of junk that she would just as soon throw in the trash. But along comes another lady who spies the lamp. In her estimation, the light fixture is the most beautiful she has ever seen. She begins to dig through her purse hoping she has enough money to buy this treasure.

What made the difference in the value each woman placed on the lamp? It wasn't something in the lamp itself, but something in each of them—the esteem in which each held it. Similarly, God considered us worth the death of His Son. He was willing to pay the price of the Blood of Jesus Christ because He loves us and wants to have us as members of His family.

26

"Or don't you know that your body is the temple of the Holy Spirit who lives in you and was given to you by God? You do not belong to yourself, for God bought you with a high price. So you must honor God with your body" (1 Corinthians 6:19-20, NLT).

"For you know that God paid a ransom to save you... And the ransom he paid was not mere gold or silver. He paid for you with the precious lifeblood of Christ, the sinless, spotless Lamb of God" (1 Peter 1:18-19, NLT).

We wrestle with the *why* question, in part, because we hope that understanding why something happened will give the event meaning and assure us that our life has value. Always remember that your worth and significance come from the fact that you are loved by God, you've been purchased by Him and, as His son or daughter, you are part of His eternal plan.

PAUL AND THE LOVE OF GOD

If troubling, anguishing circumstances prove that the Lord's love for us has diminished, then God couldn't stand the Apostle Paul. When we examine Paul's life, we see that he experienced extreme difficulties from the time he became a Christian until he was martyred for his faith. He faced tribulation, persecution, hunger, the constant threat of death, harassment from the devil and worries about the churches he oversaw (2 Corinthians 11:23-29).

Yet, when we read Paul's writings, there is no hint of: "Why is God doing this to me?" "What have I done wrong?" "God must not love me." Paul understood that the hardships he endured were not expressions of the degree of God's love for

27

him. He knew God cared for him because he recognized that the Cross of Christ was the highest demonstration of God's love. This was Paul's own testimony.

"I am living by faith, the faith of the Son of God, who in love for me, gave himself up for me" (Galatians 2:20, The New Testament in Basic English).

"Who can separate us from the love of Christ? Can trouble, pain or persecution? Can lack of clothes and food, danger to life and limb, the threat of force of arms? ...No, in all these things we win an overwhelming victory through him who has proved his love for us" (Romans 8:35-37, J.B. Phillips).

Many of the verses cited so far in this book come from portions of scripture written by Paul. Not only do they help us accurately answer the *why* question, they provide insight into how Paul viewed the numerous adversities he experienced.

- Paul knew God's love for him was not a response to his behavior. He understood that God loved him even when he was a sinner—an enemy of God who persecuted Christians (Romans 5:8-10; 1 Timothy 1:15-16).

- Paul knew his trials did not come from God. He recognized that life is hard because Adam's sin introduced a curse of death into the earth (Romans 5:12; 8:19-21).

- Paul knew men are born with sin natures and the devil works in and through them to cause much of life's chaos (Romans 5:19; Ephesians 2:1-3). He knew the devil harasses people and presents lies about God in an attempt to undermine our faith in Him (2 Corinthians 11:3; 12:7; Ephesians 6:11-12).

Paul recognized that these factors produce life's struggles. But he also understood that God is able to use these adversities and cause them to serve His plan for good as He gathers His family. Paul is the one who wrote:

"And we know that God causes everything to work together for the good of those who love God and are called according to his purpose for them. For God knew his people in advance, and he chose them to become like his Son, so that his Son would be the firstborn, with many brothers and sisters. And having chosen them, he called them to come to him. And he gave them right standing with himself, and he promised them his glory" (Romans 8:28-30, NLT).

Paul also was aware that in light of God's plan for man and the lengths to which He went to accomplish that plan, the Lord was for him. If God was for him, nothing could be permanently against him.

"What can we say about such wonderful things as these? If God is for us, who can ever be against us? Since God did not spare even his own Son but gave him up for us all, won't God, who gave us Christ, also give us everything else?" (Romans 8:31-32, NLT).

Paul understood the big picture. He knew that God, in His love, had met his greatest need—salvation from his sins—and would take care of everything else. This knowledge lightened the load of Paul's very difficult life. He wrote:

"For our present troubles are quite small and won't last very long. Yet they produce for us an immeasurably great glory that will last forever! So we don't look at the troubles we can see right now; rather, we look forward to what we have not yet seen. For the troubles we see will soon be over, but the joys to come will last forever" (2 Corinthians 4:17-18, NLT).

The great apostle understood that God's main goal right now is not to eradicate the troubles of life. Rather, God's purpose is to bring all men to salvation from their sins and make them His sons through faith in Christ. In the context of God causing sinful human choice to serve His ultimate aim, Paul declared:

"Oh, what a wonderful God we have! How great are his riches and wisdom and knowledge! How impossible it is for us to understand his decisions and his methods" (Romans 11:33, NLT).

In eternity, when we see the whole picture and have all the facts, we too will be awed by God's wisdom and purpose. We'll see how He used the realities of life in a sin cursed earth and worked out His plan to have a family.

· ⟶⟫⟫⟩ · ⟨⟨⟨⟵ ·

God loves us, not because we are good, but because He is love. God has the same love for us that He has for Jesus, His Perfect Son. The night before Jesus went to the Cross, He prayed to His Father and ours, *"that the world will know you sent me and will understand that you love them as much as you love me"* (John 17:23, TLB).

Do you want to know if God loves you or not? Don't look at your circumstances. Look at the Cross where Almighty God expressed His great unchanging love for you. Then, with the awareness that God is for you, you can face the hardships of life in a fallen world. You can be assured that God will cause your troubles to serve His eternal purposes and bring great good out of all of them.

GOD LOVES HIS SONS AND DAUGHTERS

*G*od clearly expressed His unconditional love for us through the Cross of Christ. But many of the things Jesus did and said prior to His crucifixion also give insight into God's regard for humanity. His actions and words help us understand the connection between God's love and challenging circumstances. Let's look at a few examples.

MEALTIME WITH SINNERS

When Jesus was on earth, He often ate with publicans (Jewish tax collectors) and sinners. At that time in their culture, sharing a meal meant more than simply eating with someone. It symbolized entering into relationship with that person. By eating with sinners and publicans, Jesus demonstrated that these people mattered to Him and to His Heavenly Father. The religious leaders of the day found Jesus' behavior shocking and regularly criticized Him for dining with sinners.

> *"But the Pharisees and the teachers of the law muttered, 'This man welcomes sinners and eats with them'"* (Luke 15:2, NIV).

On the particular occasion just quoted, Jesus answered the Pharisees' criticisms by telling several parables (Luke 15:4-10). In the first parable, a man lost a sheep and, in the second, a woman lost a coin. In each story, the owners searched diligently until they found their missing possessions and then rejoiced greatly when they recovered them. As Jesus spoke, He connected His questionable dining companions to the lost items. He made it clear that lost items—the kind of people He was eating with—don't lose their value when they are missing. You don't give up on them because they are gone. You search for them until you find them. Then you rejoice.

> *"I tell you that it is the same in Heaven—there is more joy over one sinner whose heart is changed than over ninety-nine righteous people who have no need for repentance* (Luke 15:7, J.B. Phillips).

Not long after this incident, critics reproved Jesus again for eating at the home of a publican. This time, Jesus plainly declared that He had come *"to seek and save that which was lost"* (Luke 19:10).

Notice that both times in response to the Pharisees' criticisms, Jesus referred to sinners as *lost*. Why? Because men in their rebellious condition are lost to the purpose for which they were created: sonship and relationship with God. When God made Adam, he made a son and a race of sons in him (Luke 3:38; Genesis 5:1-2). Adam chose independence from God when he disobeyed Him. In doing so, Adam took himself and the entire human race that was resident in him into sin and death. The Lord lost His family.

Jesus came to earth to seek and save lost humanity. He went to the Cross to pay for sin and to open the way so that

34

God could do what He always intended—transform sinful men and women into holy sons and daughters and live in loving relationship with them. Heaven rejoices over a lost sinner who repents because he is restored to his created purpose through faith in Christ.

WHEN LOST SONS COME HOME

The day that Jesus told the parables about the missing sheep and coin, He also told a third story about a missing son. The first and second parables emphasized God's mission to seek lost men. In the third account, the emphasis changed to what happens when a lost man is found. This story is commonly known as the Parable of the Prodigal Son (Luke 15:11-32).

According to Jesus, a wealthy man had two sons. The younger son demanded his inheritance and shortly after receiving it, left home. He traveled to a distant country where he spent all his money on wild, sinful living. When a severe famine hit the land, the son ended up groveling in a pigpen with a herd of swine that had more to eat than he did. In the pigpen, this wayward fellow had a change of heart.

"When he came to his senses, he said, 'How many of my father's hired men have food to spare, and here I am starving to death! I will set out and go back to my father and say to him: Father, I have sinned against heaven and against you. I am no longer worthy to be called your son; make me like one of your hired men.' So he got up and went to his father" (Luke 15:17-20, NIV).

"But, while he was still a long way off, his father saw him and was filled with compassion for him; he ran

35

to his son, threw his arms around him and kissed him. The son said to him, 'Father, I have sinned against heaven and against you. I am no longer worthy to be called your son.' But the father said to his servants, 'Quick! Bring the best robe and put it on him. Put a ring on his finger and sandals on his feet. Bring the fattened calf and kill it. Let's have a feast and celebrate. For this son of mine was dead and is alive again; he was lost and is found.' So they began to celebrate" (Luke 15:20-24, NIV).

Notice how the father dealt with his returning son. He saw his son coming when he was still some distance from the house. The father had been watching for him and was moved with compassion when he spied the lad. His heart yearned for his son. The man ran to greet him, showing an eagerness to be restored to his boy. Then he kissed him. The original language has the idea that the father expressed great tenderness and affection by kissing his son again and again. The son's reprehensible behavior had not cost him his father's love. Keep in mind that this is the dirty, stinky son—fresh from the pigpen—who wasted his father's money on prostitutes and riotous living. He was the kind of dining companion that led the Pharisees to censor Jesus.

The prodigal son wanted to talk about his sin. But the father made no mention of his many transgressions. The man knew his son was sorry for what he had done. The Pharisees who were listening to Jesus tell this story would have been horrified at the father's silence. They didn't forgive until there was revenge and restitution.

Then the father commanded the servants to give his son a robe, ring and shoes. Those who heard Jesus relate this parable would have been familiar with the writings of the prophet Zechariah. He recorded a vision God gave him where a change of clothes meant removal of sin (Zechariah 3:4). Jesus' audience knew that rings were given to men as a mark of dignity and honor. His listeners also were aware that shoes were a symbol of freedom. When prisoners of war were released, their shoes, which had been removed during captivity, were returned. Through His words, Jesus described a sinful son being fully restored to his sonship position because of his father's love.

Remember the reason Jesus told this parable—to answer the Pharisees who criticized Him for associating with sinners. Jesus' message was clear. Every publican and every sinner whom Jesus associated with during His time on earth had value to the Lord. Jesus, who *is* God and *shows* us God, had come to seek and save each one of them. Although they were lost in the pigpen of sin, these individuals were created and loved by God. They had the potential to be transformed into blameless sons and daughters through the power of the Cross.

I am not implying that all people are God's children regardless of their behavior or beliefs. All are God's creation with the *possibility* of becoming His sons, but all are guilty of sin. To realize their potential, men and women must come back to Father's house through repentance from sin and faith in Christ and His sacrifice on the Cross. Otherwise, they'll be lost forever to their created purpose and eternally separated from God.

Our journey into the pigpen of sin and rebellion has not cost us God's love. Jesus' words and actions in His earth ministry and at the Cross make it clear: Even though you are in the pigpen, I love you. If you will come back to Father's house through believing on Me, I'll clean you up. I'll clothe you with

My robe of righteousness. I'll restore you to the position of sonship, honor and dignity for which I created you.

I'VE COME BACK HOME. WHY DO I STILL HAVE PROBLEMS?

Perhaps you're thinking: "I've left the pigpen. I've come back to Father's house through faith in Christ. So why am I having all these troubles?" Because that's life in a sin cursed earth. Although our hearts have left the pigpen, we still live in a fallen world and must deal with all the issues engendered by such an environment. God eventually will cleanse the world of every trace of sin and the corruption it produces when Jesus returns. But this is not His main concern right now. God's primary intention in this present age is to draw men's hearts back to submission and dependence on Him, not to make life better in the pigsty.

Notice that the prodigal's father did not clean up the pigpen or relieve his son's suffering while he was away. This did not mean he didn't love his son. But the father's goal was not that the prodigal experience a wonderful, carefree life apart from him. His desire was that his son come back home.

Clearly, the consequences of his rebellious actions woke the son up. Jesus said the prodigal came to his senses in the pigsty. If his father had renovated the pigpen before the young man saw his true condition, his thinking may never have changed. Cleaning up the mess would have masked the fruit of the rebellious son's sin.

God currently is not cleansing and improving the muck and mud of life in this world, in part, because He wants mankind to see the destructive consequences of sin. Although the Lord takes no pleasure in people's suffering, His hope is that men and women will wake up and turn back to Him before they experience ultimate destruction—eternal separation from God in Hell.

· ➤➤➤▸ · ◂◂◂◂ ·

At this point, you may ask: "I understand that God is not behind the mayhem in this life and that He's not going to put an end to it until Jesus comes again. But does that mean He has no help for me now?"

Not at all. However, to access the power and provision of Father's house in this fallen world, you must understand what God does in the midst of circumstances that arise in the pigpen. Then you can cooperate with Him as He works. We'll discuss how He works as we answer the *what* question in the next few chapters.

THE *WHAT* QUESTION

ot only do individuals struggle with "Why did this happen?" but they also wrestle with "What is God doing?" Sadly, there is much misinformation about how God works in and through life's challenges. In this section, we will identify inaccurate answers to the *what* question and then provide correct answers from the Bible.

WRONG ANSWER: GOD SPEAKS THROUGH CIRCUMSTANCES

Many people believe that God imparts information to us through our physical circumstances. So they look at their predicament and draw conclusions based on what they see. However, you cannot answer the *why* or *what* questions by observing your situation.

- Since difficult circumstances are not orchestrated by God, we can be certain that He is not sending us a message through them.

- God has told us to *"walk by faith...not by sight or appearance"* (2 Corinthians 5:7, AMP). If God

41

attempted to disclose information and direction through what we see in our situation, He would contradict His instruction to us.

- God speaks to us through His written Word. His Word is a lamp to our feet and a light to our path (Psalm 119:105). *"My son, keep your father's [God-given] commandment, and forsake not the law of [God] your mother [taught you]...When you go, [the Word of your parents' God] it shall lead you; when you sleep, it shall keep you, and when you waken, it shall talk with you. For the commandment is a lamp, and the whole teaching of the law is light"* (Proverbs 6:20-23, AMP).

The Bible mentions a number of cases where people tried to address the *what* question by looking at their circumstances. In each case, they drew erroneous conclusions. Such an incident occurred when the Apostle Paul was shipwrecked and he and his shipmates swam safely to a nearby island.

"Once we were safe on shore, we learned that we were on the island of Malta. The people of the island were very kind to us. It was cold and rainy, so they built a fire on the shore to welcome us and warm us. As Paul gathered an armful of sticks and was laying them on the fire, a poisonous snake, driven out by the heat, fastened itself onto his hand. The people of the island saw it hanging there and said to each other, 'A murderer, no doubt! Though he escaped the sea, justice will not permit him to live.' But Paul shook off the snake into the fire and was unharmed. The people waited for him to swell up or suddenly drop dead. But when they had waited a long time and saw no harm

come to him, they changed their minds and decided he was a god" (Acts 28:1-6, NLT).

These islanders saw Paul escape drowning in the sea, but then watched a deadly snake bite him. They reasoned that he was a murderer who beat death by surviving the shipwreck, yet the snake bite proved that justice had now caught up with him. However, when Paul was unaffected by the serpent's venom, the islanders then decided that he must be a god. In a matter of minutes, these people came to two very different conclusions about Paul and what happened based on what they could see— and neither deduction was correct.

That's how some individuals live their lives. They presume that each change in their plight is God's way of communicating with them. Consider this example: A loved one lies in a hospital bed. His blood pressure goes up too high and the family asks: "What is God saying?" "What is God doing?" Then the man's blood pressure drops too low and his family reacts with: "What is the Lord trying to show us now?" God isn't trying to reveal anything through this hospital scene. Their loved one's unstable blood pressure is not a message from the Lord. It is the product of life in a sin cursed earth.

Consider another case. When Joshua led the Hebrew people into Canaan, God commanded them not to make treaties with any tribes in the region. As Israel began to conquer and settle the land, one particular group, the Gibeonites, decided to use deception to save themselves. Although they lived nearby, they sent ambassadors to Joshua who were dressed and outfitted as though they had traveled many miles.

"They...(loaded) their donkeys with weathered saddlebags and old patched wineskins. They put on

ragged clothes and worn-out, patched sandals. And they took along dry, moldy bread for provisions. When they arrived at the camp of Israel at Gilgal, they told Joshua and the men of Israel, 'We have come from a distant land to ask you to make a peace treaty with us'" (Joshua 9:4-6, NLT).

The leaders of Israel examined the material evidence presented to them, accepted the story told by the men, and entered into a binding agreement with the Gibeonites—just what God told them *not* to do. Note that the leaders assessed their situation based on what they saw instead of seeking God's Word: *"So the Israelite leaders examined their bread, but they did not consult the Lord"* (Joshua 9:14, NLT). In this incident, we again see that physical data can give inaccurate information and mislead God's own people.

You cannot appraise your situation in terms of what you see and feel. The Bible is the only fully reliable source of information we have about God and how He works. You must judge your circumstances according to what God says in His written Word. We'll look at some examples in later chapters that reveal how God works in life's hardships. They will help us rightly assess our own situations.

WRONG ANSWER: CIRCUMSTANCES SHOW US GOD'S WILL

Others believe that God makes His will known through physical circumstances. They're convinced that if an event takes place, it must be God's will. Yet, all sorts of things happen in this life that are not the will of God. Some things come about because the devil is trying to steal, kill and destroy men. Others happen because men rebel against God and commit

44

reprehensible acts. And some hardships are the result of random processes at work in this sin cursed earth. (Review Chapter 1, if necessary.)

Several years ago, I participated in a home Bible study. Two young ladies decided to attend one evening, but never arrived. They later said they couldn't find the house, which, in their minds, meant it wasn't God's will for them to participate in the study. However, their inability to find the house was not an expression of the Lord's will. Either these women weren't skilled at following directions or they made a wrong turn on the way to the house.

It's a good thing a man named Onesiphorus didn't use his physical situation to determine God's will. Doing so would have kept him from being a tremendous blessing to the Apostle Paul when Paul was jailed in Rome.

> *"May the Lord show special kindness to Onesiphorus and all his family because he often visited and encouraged me. He was never ashamed of me because I was in prison. When he came to Rome, **he searched everywhere until he found me"** (2 Timothy 1:16-17, NLT).

Notice that Onesiphorus had to scour the city to find Paul. Had he assessed his circumstances the same way as the young women mentioned above, he wouldn't have located Paul. Onesiphorus would have given up when he didn't find Paul in the first place he looked, believing that it wasn't God's will for him to locate the apostle.

God leads us by His Spirit in line with His written Word. But that's a lesson for another day. The current point is this: You cannot look at your circumstances to answer the *what* question. You have to look at the information in the Bible to find out what God does and how He works in life's events.

WRONG ANSWER: GOD WORKS ON US THROUGH CIRCUMSTANCES

Some individuals believe that God works *on* us through circumstances, but this isn't accurate. Nowhere does the Bible say that God works on us. Instead, scripture says God works *in* us by His Spirit and His Word. Consider these passages.

> *"Being confident of this, that he who began a good work in you will carry it on to completion until the day of Christ Jesus"* (Philippians 1:6, NIV).

> *"Continue to work out your salvation with fear and trembling, for it is God who works in you to will and to act according to his good purpose"* (Philippians 2:12-13, NIV).

> *"May the God of peace...equip you with everything good for doing his will, and may he work in us what is pleasing to him, through Jesus Christ"* (Hebrews 13:20-21, NIV).

> *"And all of us, as with unveiled face, [because we] continued to behold [**in the Word of God**] as in a mirror the glory of the Lord, are constantly being transfigured into His very own image in ever increasing splendor and from one degree of glory to another; [for this comes]*

from the Lord [Who is] the Spirit" (2 Corinthians 3:18, AMP).

*"And as the Spirit of the Lord works **within** us, we become more and more like him and reflect his glory even more"* (2 Corinthians 3:18, NLT).

*"And we will never stop thanking God that when we preached his message to you, you didn't think of the words we spoke as being just our own. You accepted what we said as the very word of God—which, of course, it was. And this word continues to work **in** you who believe"* (1 Thessalonians 2:13, NLT).

If you think God works on you through outside forces, you'll constantly look at your environment to figure out what God is doing and you'll draw erroneous conclusions, like the people mentioned in the previous section.

You may wonder: "Doesn't God orchestrate or allow difficult circumstances to test us, teach us, purge us and perfect us?" God does indeed test, teach, purge and perfect us, but He does so by His Word and His Spirit working in us, not through difficult circumstances. (For a complete review of each of these points, read *God is Good and Good Means Good.*)

Now that we have addressed some incorrect answers to the *what* question, let's answer the question according to the Bible.

THE CORRECT ANSWER TO THE *WHAT* QUESTION

*J*ust because circumstances don't tell us what God is doing doesn't mean we can't know—the Bible tells us. It may not give specific details about a particular circumstance, but as we study God's Word, we can see general principles by which God works in every situation.

The Bible is filled with accounts of God moving in hard times to bring about tremendous results—great glory to Himself, much good to as many people as possible, and real good out of truly evil events. In these narratives, we see God working according to the following precepts:

- Much of God's work is invisible until you finally see visible results. Just because you can't see anything happening doesn't mean that nothing is happening.

- The Lord does things at the right time.

- He often puts off short-term blessing (ending the trouble immediately) for long-term, eternal results as He uses human choice and causes it to serve His purposes.

- God brings genuine good out of genuine bad.

- He will get you through until He gets you out. God can even cause you to thrive in the midst of very difficult circumstances.

JESUS SHOWS US HOW GOD WORKS

Jesus' response in certain situations gives us insight into how God works. When we observe what Jesus (God in human flesh) did, we see these principles in operation.

A good example is seen in one of the instances where Jesus multiplied loaves and fish. Scripture says that a huge crowd of five thousand men, plus women and children, had followed Jesus all day long.

> *"That evening the disciples came to him and said, 'This is a desolate place, and it is getting late. Send the crowds away so they can go to the villages and buy food for themselves.' But Jesus replied, 'That isn't necessary—you feed them'"* (Matthew 14:15-16, NLT).

The disciples did not have provision for such a multitude. Consequently, they faced lack. This brings up the *why* question. "Why is there lack in this world?" Insufficient food is part of the curse in the earth brought about by Adam's sin. "Why was there shortage on that particular day?" Because no one had brought food with them to compensate for the lack of supplies in the area.

"When Jesus then lifted up his eyes, and saw a great company come unto him, he saith unto Philip, Whence shall we buy bread that these may eat? And this he **said** *to* **prove** *him: for he himself knew what he would do"* (John 6:5-6).

Although Jesus was in no way behind this insufficiency, He saw a way to use it for the good of His twelve disciples. Jesus had previously taught them that they have a Father in Heaven who gives provision to His children when they seek Him. His question gave Philip and the other disciples an opportunity to demonstrate and strengthen their faith in God and His promise. They could have answered: "We don't know where we'll get the food, but we're certain that our Heavenly Father will help us."

Many people mistakenly believe that God orchestrates the difficulties of life to test us. But God's test is never the circumstance itself. Instead, His test is His Word in the *midst* of the situation. Jesus tested His disciples in this incident with His words: Will you believe what I have told you about your Father in the face of this great lack?

The disciples made the same mistake many people make when confronted with challenging circumstances—they didn't remember Jesus' past instructions. They tried to figure out a solution to their troubles by looking at what they could see and then drawing conclusions.

"Philip replied, 'It would take a small fortune to feed them!' Then Andrew, Simon Peter's brother, spoke up. 'There's a young boy here with five barley loaves and two fish. But what good is that with this huge crowd?'" (John 6:7-8, NLT).

Philip began to think in terms of how they could meet the need if they had enough money. Andrew reasoned away what would actually become the solution to the problem—a little boy's lunch. Neither one thought of their Father's promise to help them.

GOD KNOWS WHAT HE IS DOING

Jesus already knew what He intended to do when He asked Philip how they would provide bread for the crowd. However, He didn't tell His disciples what He had in mind. Even though the disciples didn't know the specific actions the Lord would take, they could have rested on the fact that God always knows what He's going to do, even if He doesn't give us the exact details.

Also notice that even though Jesus planned to meet the need, He didn't provide food immediately. Why? Because God does things at the *right time*, not necessarily *right now*. Jesus instructed the disciples to seat everyone on the grass in the area. No doubt, it took some time to seat ten thousand people. When everyone was settled, Jesus took the young boy's bread and fish and gave thanks to the Father. Then He handed the lad's lunch to His disciples who distributed the food to those who sat on the hillsides.

"'Tell everyone to sit down,' Jesus ordered. So all of them—the men alone numbered five thousand— sat down on the grassy slopes. Then Jesus took the loaves, gave thanks to God, and passed them out to the people. Afterward he did the same with the fish. And they all ate until they were full" (John 6:10-11, NLT).

"'Now gather the leftovers,' Jesus told his disciples, 'so that nothing is wasted.' There were only five barley loaves to start with, but twelve baskets were filled with the pieces of bread the people did not eat" (John 6:12-13, NLT).

Consider what happened here and what this account shows us about how God works. Jesus took the five loaves and two fish—clearly not enough food to feed almost ten thousand people—and thanked His Father. Even though lack doesn't come from God, Jesus thanked Him for it. Why did He do that? Because He knew that *not enough* would become *more than enough* in the hands of His Father. He knew that God would bring genuine good (full provision) out of genuine bad (insufficient food).

Why did Jesus take the time to make everyone sit down? Why didn't He just pray over the food and pass it out? Jesus wanted everyone seated so all could see that only a little food was available and all could see Him acknowledge His Father. Since everything was done in an orderly manner, everyone saw what happened. Food that should have quickly run out did not. Everybody knew that God had worked a miracle.

Even though the disciples didn't see immediate results when they came to Jesus with their problem, it didn't mean that nothing was happening. Jesus had a plan and things were falling into place. When the results were finally visible, God received the highest glory and as many people as possible were helped and blessed.

God's provision and deliverance are not always instantaneous, not because God wants people to suffer, but because He sees that the passage of time will maximize the situation. It will bring Him more glory and more good to more people. Keep in mind that even though these people had to wait to eat, no one starved, all got plenty, and there was even enough left over for some to-go boxes.

GOD AT WORK

Jesus is God and shows us God, so when we look at how He handled this circumstance, we get insight into how God works and what He does in the midst of life's hardships. This information can help us answer the *what* question as we face life's trials.

Just because you can't figure out a solution to your troubles doesn't mean that God has no plan. And just because you don't see anything happening in your situation doesn't mean that nothing is happening. God knew about the challenges you would face before He formed the earth and He already has a strategy in mind to cause them to serve His purposes of maximum glory and maximum good. He is at work behind the scenes.

That's what's happening. That's the answer to the *what* question.

The next two chapters will help us further understand the correct answer to the *why* and *what* questions. We'll look at real people who experienced genuine adversities. When we study their stories, we will see how God worked in their lives by the principles that Jesus demonstrated when He helped His disciples in their time of need.

JOSEPH'S STORY

*J*oseph's story is an example of what the Lord does with life's challenges. God brought maximum glory to Himself and maximum good to multitudes as He worked in Joseph's circumstances according to the principles mentioned in the previous chapter. Let's look at what God did.

WHAT HAPPENED TO JOSEPH?

Jacob, the son of Abraham, fathered twelve sons. Joseph, the eleventh son, was Jacob's favorite. When Joseph was a young man, God promised him greatness. This promise, combined with his father's favor, made his brothers hate him.

When Joseph was seventeen, his brothers plotted to kill him but changed their minds and sold him into slavery instead. Slave traders took Joseph to Egypt. Potiphar, an officer of Pharaoh—king of Egypt—purchased Joseph and gave Joseph command of his household. While there, Potiphar's wife falsely accused Joseph of rape and he was sent to prison.

Joseph met two other captives in prison, a butler and a baker who worked for Pharaoh. They were imprisoned because they had offended their king. Over time, both men had dreams they did not understand, but Joseph was able to explain them. According to Joseph's interpretations, the baker would be hanged and the butler would be restored to his butlership. Joseph's predictions came to pass. The baker died and the butler was reinstated.

The butler forgot about Joseph for two years until Pharaoh had dreams that no one could interpret. On the word of the butler, Pharaoh summoned Joseph to court, where Joseph correctly interpreted the dreams as warnings of a coming famine. The dreams predicted seven years of great abundance followed by seven years of great lack. In response to Joseph's interpretations, Pharaoh put him in charge of storing food before the famine began and then distributing the goods during the lean time. Joseph was thirty years old at this point.

Joseph successfully designed and implemented the gathering and distribution programs. When Egypt and the surrounding nations faced the famine, there was plenty of food to feed those who were affected. Joseph's own brothers were among those who came to him for help. He eventually was reunited with his family when his father, brothers, and their wives and children moved to Egypt to live. Joseph's complete story is recorded in Genesis 37—50.

WHY DID THIS HAPPEN?

Joseph's tribulations bring up the *why* question. Why did this happen to him? We know that God was not the source of Joseph's troubles. First, Jesus—who *is* God and *shows us* God—never treated anyone like Joseph's brothers treated him. Therefore, Joseph's trials could not have been the work of God. Second, the Lord ultimately delivered him from his afflictions (Acts 7:9-10). God does not afflict people, directly or indirectly, only to turn around and deliver them. This would be a house divided against itself.

Joseph's experience has Satan's fingerprints all over it. The Bible says that the devil is a murderer and liar who seeks to steal from and devour men (John 8:44; John 10:10; 1 Peter 5:8). This is exactly what Joseph's brothers did to him. They plotted to murder him, then sold him into slavery and lied to their father about what happened. Potiphar's wife also lied about Joseph and, as a result, stole years of his life.

Did Satan directly orchestrate Joseph's ordeal? The Bible doesn't say this was the case and it really doesn't matter. As we mentioned in Chapter 1, Satan works on men in an attempt to affect their behavior. The devil had access to Joseph's brothers and all the people along the way through their fallen natures and unrenewed minds.

A series of freewill acts carried out by fallen people influenced by Satan caused Joseph's misfortunes. These troubles beset him because that's life in a sin cursed earth.

WHAT WAS GOD DOING?

We can see from Joseph's story how God maximized the consequences of human choice for His glory and much good, even choices He did not approve of or orchestrate. But timing was involved. God put off short-term blessing (ending Joseph's problems the day they started) for long-term eternal results. Consider these examples:

- God could have clearly warned Joseph what his brothers intended to do but, as far as we know, He did not. That information would not have solved Joseph's problems. The brothers still had hatred and murder in their hearts toward him, which made future trouble likely.

• Had God intervened at that point, Joseph would not have ended up in Egypt in charge of a food distribution program and he and his family may not have survived the famine. Had they been wiped out, it would have thwarted God's plan for a family of sons and daughters through Christ since Jesus came into the world through Joseph's family (Abraham's descendants).

• God did not step in when Potiphar's wife lied about Joseph because He could see where her choices would lead. Joseph was incarcerated due to her lie. But it was in prison that he met the butler, who was Joseph's link to Pharaoh.

• The butler was eventually released from prison. However, two years passed before he remembered to speak to Pharaoh about Joseph. Had the case come before Pharaoh prior to the king's puzzling dreams, Joseph might have been released from prison, but there would have been no reason to promote him. He may have faded into obscurity in Egypt or returned to Canaan and possibly died in the famine. Either way, he would not have been put in charge of the food program.

God brought great good out of the evil done to Joseph. He ended up positioned to feed his family and, as a result, was able to preserve the line through which Jesus would one day come. Joseph's plan spared many thousands of others from starvation and multitudes heard about the One True God as he acknowledged the Lord through his adversities. For instance:

- During Joseph's servitude in Potiphar's house, Potiphar, a worshipper of the gods of Egypt, realized that the Almighty God was with Joseph (Genesis 39:3).

- While Joseph was in prison, he acknowledged God as the One who gave him accurate interpretations of the baker's and butler's dreams. Consequently, many more Egyptian idol worshippers heard about the Only All-Powerful God (Genesis 40:8).

- Joseph again gave credit to the Lord when he was able to interpret Pharaoh's troubling dreams. The king recognized that God was at work: "(Joseph) *is a man who is obviously filled with the spirit of God* (Genesis 41:38-39, NLT).

- Many countries came to Egypt for food during the years of famine. Great numbers of these people likely heard about the Sovereign Lord as they were told why Egypt had plenty of food when no one else did (Genesis 41:57).

God never abandoned Joseph during his ordeal. Instead, He preserved Joseph and caused him to thrive in the midst of very difficult circumstances. Note these examples:

- Joseph quickly advanced when he arrived at Potiphar's house as a slave. Potiphar gave Joseph charge over the entire household. *"But the Lord was with Joseph, and he [though a slave] was a successful and prosperous*

man...(he) *found favor in his* (Potiphar's) *sight...*
And [his master] made him supervisor over his house
and he put all that he had in his (Joseph's) *charge"*
(Genesis 39:2-4, AMP).

- Death was the standard penalty for rape. Although
  Joseph was accused of this crime, Pharaoh sentenced
  him to prison for political captives instead of
  execution.

- Joseph was placed in irons in prison. But God delivered
  him from these chains and put him in a position of
  great responsibility—charge over the entire prison.
  And when Pharaoh's butler and baker arrived, Joseph
  personally waited on them.

- After Joseph interpreted Pharaoh's dreams, Pharaoh
  promoted Joseph to second-in-command in Egypt.
  Pharaoh told him, *"Only I will have a rank higher
  than yours"* (Genesis 41:40, NLT).

JOSEPH'S VIEW OF HIS TRIALS

Pharaoh also gave Joseph a wife and he raised a family
in Egypt. The names of Joseph's children give us great insight
into what Joseph thought of God's help and provision throughout
his difficulties.

*"Joseph named his older son Manasseh, for he said,
'God has made me forget all my troubles and the
family of my father.' Joseph named his second son*

*Ephraim, for he said, 'God has made me fruitful in
this land of my suffering'"* (Genesis 41:51-52, NLT).

Every time Joseph uttered the names of his children, he
proclaimed that God had taken away the painful memories of
his hardship and loss and given him a life of abundance in what
had been a land of suffering. Joseph had such peace and victory
in his situation that when his brothers came to Egypt for food,
he was able to tell them:

> "(God) *sent me here ahead of you to preserve your
> lives...to keep you and your families alive so that you
> will become a great nation"* (Genesis 45:5-7, NLT).

When Joseph said God *sent* him to Egypt, he didn't mean
that God *caused* his troubles. Rather, he expressed how *in
control* God is of His universe and human choice. God didn't
cause any of it, but He used all of it. By this, I mean, God knew
what the brothers were going to do to Joseph before they did
it and He worked their choices into His plan. Joseph's brothers
perpetrated great evil against him when they sold him into
slavery. But God used their wicked choice to ultimately bring
Joseph to a position of power in Egypt. As a result, countless
lives were saved and thousands of people heard about Jehovah,
the One True God. That's how *in control* God was and is.

As he looked back on his experiences, Joseph could clearly
see that God is so great, He can take wicked actions not of His
doing and cause them to serve His purposes. At the end of it all,
Joseph was able to declare to his brothers:

> *"As far as I am concerned, God turned into good
> what you meant for evil. He brought me to the high*

61

position I have today so I could save the lives of many people" (Genesis 50:20, NLT).

› →➤➤➤ · ◀◀◀◀← ‹

What did God do in Joseph's life? He worked behind the scenes and caused the choices of men to serve His purposes. God's timing was perfect. He put off short-term blessing (immediate deliverance) for long-term eternal results. God got Joseph through until He got him out and caused Joseph to flourish under very severe conditions. The Lord brought genuine good out of genuine evil and maximum glory to Himself, as well as maximum good to untold numbers of men and women as He worked out His eternal plan of salvation.

That's the answer to the *what* question in Joseph's story.

THE STORY OF MOSES AND ISRAEL

The story of Moses and the Hebrew people who left
Egypt and journeyed back to their homeland in Canaan gives
us more insight into how God works in life's trials. In this
account, we see God doing for them the kinds of things He did
for Joseph.

THE STORY BEGINS

In Joseph's day, the fledgling nation of Israel—seventy-five
people in all—went down to Egypt for food during the famine.
They settled there and prospered greatly. As time passed,
Joseph and his generation died off, but their descendants had
many children and grandchildren. *In fact, they multiplied so
quickly that they soon filled the land"* (Exodus 1:7, NLT). The
Egyptians reacted to this rapid growth with fear. When a new
king came to power who knew nothing about Joseph or his
deeds, he ruthlessly enslaved the Hebrew people.

God's people fell into slavery because that's life in a
sin cursed earth. It is the nature of fallen men to rule over other
men. The devil works through that inclination and influences
men to enslave each other. In this damaged world, the freewill

choices of fallen men influenced by Satan can produce calamitous consequences. This is what happened to Israel.

The Israelites continued to grow despite harsh living conditions. So Pharaoh ordered the Hebrew midwives and his own people to destroy Israel's newborn boys. *"But the more the Egyptians oppressed them, **the more quickly the Israelites multiplied"** (Exodus 1:12, NLT). God can cause His people to prosper even in very challenging circumstances.

During this period, Moses was born to a Hebrew couple. They hid him for three months to prevent him from being killed. When his parents could no longer hide him, they placed their trust in God and put him into a small waterproof basket on the Nile River. Pharaoh's daughter found Moses among the reeds along the river's edge and decided to adopt him as her son. Moses' sister, Miriam, who had been watching the basket from a distance, approached the Egyptian princess and offered to find a wet nurse to feed the baby. The princess agreed and Miriam took the infant home to their mother. Moses' mother took care of her son until he was weaned. Then she turned him over to Pharaoh's daughter.

God brought real good out of genuine bad in the midst of this toilsome and dangerous environment. The Lord took the very thing that was working to destroy the Hebrew boys—Egypt—and made it the instrument He used to save Moses' life. When Pharaoh's daughter retrieved Moses out of the Nile River, he became a protected prince of Egypt. Not only did Moses survive, he had his mother's godly influence in his early years. Then when she returned Moses to the princess, as a royal son, he was given training he would not have received had he grown up among the Hebrews as a brick-making slave. *"And he became mighty in both speech and action"* (Acts 7:22, NLT).

64

When Moses reached adulthood, he felt drawn to the Israelites. But at forty years old, he killed an Egyptian who had abused a Hebrew slave. Moses fled Egypt and spent four decades in the deserts of Midian, in the land of Arabia. God did not cause Moses to kill the Egyptian and leave Egypt, but He used Moses' actions and worked them into His overall plan.

God had chosen Moses to guide the Israelites back to their homeland. Yet, the rashness of his act in killing the Egyptian showed that he was not yet ready to lead a large group of difficult people on a treacherous journey. Moses needed time to develop the character traits that would make him a great leader. That time of character development took place in Midian. It was also in Midian that Moses—who had been raised in a palace—learned to live in the desert. He received the precise training he needed to fulfill God's plan to guide his people through a desert wilderness on the way to Canaan.

THE BEST WAY THROUGH

Moses was eighty years old when he returned to Egypt to fulfill his destiny. He went to Pharaoh and demanded the release of the Hebrews from slavery. Pharaoh refused. After a series of calamities befell the Egyptians over a nine month period, Pharaoh agreed to release the Israelites and allow them to leave Egypt. Their trek back to Canaan began.

There were two routes by which God could have directed Israel home—the way of the Philistines and the wilderness route through the Sinai Peninsula (Exodus 13:17-18). The first route was populated by a warlike tribe of idol worshippers called the Philistines. The second was mountainous and dry, with peaks rising to 7,400 feet and less than 8 inches of rainfall per year.

The journey along either track was arduous due to the effects of Adam's first sin. His disobedience produced a sin nature in man that resulted in aggressive tribes bent on conquering other men—like the one along the Philistine road. The wilderness route went through the desert. Desert places and the opposition they present developed because of the curse of death that came on the earth when Adam sinned.

God did not author the challenges along either route, but He knew which path would produce maximum results. He selected the best way for Israel—the passage through the Sinai wilderness—and had a plan to use this course to bring great good to Israel and much glory to Himself.

Egypt's army was formidable and the distance between Egypt and Canaan was not that far. Once the Israelites were settled in Canaan, the Egyptian army would have been a constant source of danger to them. God saw a way to end this threat. The Lord knew that Pharaoh would change his mind about releasing the Hebrews from bondage. Pharaoh sent his army after his newly freed slaves, believing that his former captives were bogged down in the wilderness at the edge of the Red Sea. While the Egyptians pursued the Hebrews, God parted the waters of the sea and allowed Israel to walk through on dry ground. When the Egyptian warriors attempted to follow, the waters closed over them and they were destroyed.

Great good came out of this event. Not only did God remove a real threat to Israel, but the parting of the Red Sea had a tremendous impact on the Hebrews.

"When the people of Israel saw the mighty power that the Lord had displayed against the Egyptians, they

feared the Lord and put their faith in him and his servant Moses" (Exodus 14:31, NLT).

PROVISION IN THE DESERT

The Sinai wilderness passage was daunting and hazardous. Israel endured many challenges as they traveled through the desert, including lack of food and water, snakes, scorpions, heat, dirt and fatigue. But God cared for His people even in the midst of the challenges their environment presented. He got them through the desert until He got them out.

"(God) *brought his people safely out of Egypt, loaded with silver and gold; there were no sick or feeble people among them. ...The Lord spread out a cloud above them as a covering and gave them a great fire to light the darkness. They asked for meat, and he sent them quail; he gave them manna—bread from heaven. He opened up a rock, and water gushed out to form a river through the dry and barren land"* (Psalm 105:37-41, NLT).

"The Lord your God cared for you again and again here in the wilderness, just as a father cares for his child" (Deuteronomy 1:31, NLT).

"For all these forty years your clothes didn't wear out, and your feet didn't blister or swell" (Deuteronomy 8:4, NLT).

GOD'S PERFECT TIMING

The trip from Egypt to their homeland was an eleven day journey. Yet, it took Israel two years to get to Canaan

(Deuteronomy 1:2; Numbers 10:11-13). Two years for a two week trip may seem too long, but God's timing is perfect. He was at work during Israel's waiting period. Much good happened.

God met with Moses on Mount Sinai and gave him the Law that Israel was to follow once they reached the land God had promised them. Moses also received instructions for building the Tabernacle and carrying out the sacrificial system that would be vital to their spiritual life when they settled in Canaan.

The two year delay gave time for word of the Egyptian army's defeat at the hand of the God of the Hebrews to spread all the way to Canaan. By the time the Israelites reached their homeland, the tribes living there were afraid of them. This gave Israel a great strategic advantage.

Jericho was the first city the Hebrews encountered when they entered their ancestral home. Prior to an attack on the city, two spies were sent on a reconnaissance mission inside the walls of Jericho. When the king of Jericho discovered their presence in the fortress, a prostitute named Rahab hid the men and helped them escape. She explained to them why she was willing to help.

> *"We are all afraid of you. Everyone is living in terror. For we have heard how the Lord made a dry path for you through the Red Sea when you left Egypt. ...No wonder our hearts have melted in fear! No one has the courage to fight after hearing such things. For the Lord your God is the supreme God of the heavens above and the earth below"* (Joshua 2:9-11, NLT).

Not only had Israel's delay given time for fear and dread to develop among the local inhabitants, it produced eternal results. Rahab, an idol-worshipping pagan, realized that the Hebrew

God was the True God. She recognized Him to be Almighty God and, as a result, she was willing to aid the spies. Rahab is in Heaven today because Israel's arrival in the land was put off for two years. Rahab's salvation was certainly worth the wait. How many other people in Canaan came to the same realization as Rahab and abandoned their idols to serve the One True God? Only eternity will tell.

GOD USES LIFE'S CHALLENGES

Because God is sovereign, or all powerful, He is able to use circumstances not of His making and cause them to work for the good of His people. The record of Israel's trip to Canaan shows us how God does this. Consider these three points.

Faith Can Be Strengthened in Trials

Once Israel passed through the Red Sea, they journeyed three days into the desert and couldn't find water. They finally reached water at a place called Marah, but the water was undrinkable. Moses turned to the Lord for help and God directed him to throw a tree branch into the bitter pool. He obeyed and the water was made good to drink (Exodus 15:22-26).

God did not cause the situation. Clearly, it was God's will for Israel to have drinkable water because He purified the water when Moses followed His instructions. Why were the waters of Marah undrinkable? It is simply another example of how Adam's sin brought a curse that corrupted life in the earth.

God could have transformed the water before His people arrived but didn't because He saw a way to use the situation for Israel's benefit. Walled cities and formidable enemies awaited the Hebrews in the land ahead. They would need practiced, proven faith to enter in and take possession of their homeland.

The bitter waters at Marah gave the Hebrews a chance to exercise and strengthen their faith. They had an opportunity to develop their ability to walk by faith instead of sight and confidently proclaim: "We need water and don't know how we're going to get it. But we aren't worried. God will provide!"

Patience Can Be Strengthened in Trials

Due to the nature of life in a sin cursed earth, we don't always see instant deliverance from life's troubles. Therefore, we must be able to hold steady until we experience victory. That is what patience is all about—remaining steadfast despite how the situation looks.

Some mistakenly believe troubles make us patient. However, trials don't produce the ability to endure any more than exercise creates muscles. Rather, life's challenges give us an occasion to use our ability to endure by God's power in us and, consequently, our patience or endurance grows stronger. That's one way God utilizes the hardships of this life.

> *"Be assured and understand that the trial and proving of your faith **bring out** endurance and steadfastness and patience"* (James 1:3, AMP).

When you express faith and patience in the face of trouble and boldly stand your ground on God's Word, God's power strengthens you to persist until you experience His provision and deliverance. Successfully maintaining your position in one area gives you confidence that through God's help, you can endure the next challenge that life brings your way.

You don't know what's ahead as you journey through this life. The practice you're getting at walking by faith and patience in your present circumstance may be exactly what you need to overcome the next big difficulty. That was the case for the Hebrew people.

Flaws Can Be Exposed in Trials

Israel passed up the opportunity to exercise their faith and patience at Marah. Instead, they complained about the lack of drinkable water. *"So the people grumbled against Moses, saying, 'What are we to drink?'"* (Exodus 15:24, NIV).

Trials often expose character flaws in us just as the bitter pool at Marah did for Israel. Flaws can be dealt with once they are exposed. This is another way God utilizes troubles He does not orchestrate. The incident at Marah would have been a perfect time for His people to recognize and deal with their grumbling. Sadly, Israel did not acknowledge and address their sin. They continued to complain all the way to Canaan.

Complaining is a serious defect because it is the voice of unbelief. Complaining talks only about what it sees and feels. It does not take God's past help, present provision and future promises into consideration. Israel's constant grumbling strengthened their faith in what their eyes told them rather than in what God said. By the time Israel reached Canaan, they had developed a pattern of discounting God's Word and assessing their situation only in terms of what they could see. This habit of unbelief cost them the Promised Land.

When the Israelites reached the edge of Canaan, Moses sent twelve spies in to survey the land. All but two of them returned with a dire report about great walls and giant warriors.

71

As a result, the entire nation of Israel refused to cross the border even though God had promised them victory over their enemies. They lost the land that God wanted them to have.

Perhaps you're wondering why we're discussing people who did not see God's will come to pass in their lives. The fact is, we can learn from their errors. God had men record the account of Israel's journey, in part, so that we don't make the same mistakes.

"These things happened to them as examples and were written down as warnings for us, on whom the fulfillment of the ages has come" (1 Corinthians 10:11, NIV).

In the next section, we'll discuss how we can avoid Israel's failures and respond to hardships in a way that opens the door to God's help as He works in this sin cursed earth.

PART TWO:

WHAT SHOULD WE DO AND WHY?

THE APPROPRIATE RESPONSE

We have successfully answered the *why* and *what* questions in regard to God. Now we need to address these questions in connection with ourselves. In light of the challenges of life in a world damaged by sin, *what* should we do and *why*?

As we discussed in the previous section, God wants to bring maximum glory to Himself and maximum good to as many people as possible while He gathers His family for eternity. We can learn to deal with life's difficulties in cooperation with God as He works to accomplish these purposes.

RESPOND WITH JOY

The Bible prescribes very specific instructions about what we are to do in the face of adversity. James 1:2 says *"Consider it wholly joyful, my brethren, whenever you are enveloped in or encounter trials of any sort, or fall into various temptations"* (AMP). When the trials of life come our way, God's Word directs us to think of them as occasions to be joyful. To be joyful means to praise God.

To praise someone means to proclaim their virtues and accomplishments. I taught high school history for many years. From time to time, a student would exhibit character traits or scholastic accomplishments that deserved a word of praise from me. My praise had nothing to do with how I felt, if I was in a good or bad mood, or whether my life was going well or not. I commended the student because it was appropriate. In the same way, it is always appropriate to praise the Lord for who He is and what He does.

Praise to God is not an emotional response to life's hardships. Notice that the verse quoted above does not say we are to *feel* joyful. It is not humanly possible to feel good about encountering something bad. However, you can *be* joyful even when you don't *feel* joyful. In the context of the many tribulations and trials he faced in his lifetime, the Apostle Paul talked about being *"sorrowful, yet always rejoicing"* (2 Corinthians 6:10).

People sometimes balk when they are told to rejoice in the face of tribulation. They think such a response is unnatural or even ridiculous. But rejoicing must be the right thing to do because Almighty God is the one who instructs us to respond with praise. If we understand the purpose and power of praise, not only is it an act of obedience, it makes sense to do it.

PRAISE PREPARES THE WAY

The Spirit of God inspired the Psalmist David to write these intriguing words: *"Out of the mouth of babes and sucklings hast thou ordained strength because of thine enemies, that thou mightest still the enemy and the avenger"* (Psalm 8:2). According to this verse, there is a strength that can stop an adversary. Even children and nursing infants can express this strength.

Jesus identified this power as praise to God. Just a few days before He was crucified, while in the Temple at Jerusalem, He healed many blind and lame people. Some children witnessed the healings and began to cry out *"Hosanna to the Son of David!"* (Matthew 21:9). Hosanna means *"Oh save Lord."* It was an exclamation of adoration and praise. These youths were praising God for His wonderful works expressed through Jesus that day.

The chief priests and teachers of the Law of Moses were outraged and challenged Jesus, *"Do you hear what these children are saying?"* (Matthew 21:16a, NIV). He answered them by quoting David's words: *"Have ye never read, Out of the mouth of babes and sucklings thou hast perfected praise"* (Matthew 21:16b). Notice that Jesus changed the word *strength* in David's psalm to *praise.* Through His response to His critics, Jesus made it clear that praise to God is the strength that stops the enemy and stills the avenger.

Another psalmist wrote, *"Whoso offereth praise glorifieth me:* (Psalm 50:23a, KJV) *and he prepares the way so that I may show him the salvation of God"* (Psalm 50:23b, NIV). As you acknowledge and praise God in the face of adversity by praising Him—by talking about who He is and what He has done, is doing and will do—you bring glory to God and open the way for Him to demonstrate His power in your situation.

Praise glorifies the Lord because it honors Him. Praise opens the door to God's power because, by acknowledging and thanking Him for His help and provision before you see it, you are expressing faith. And God works in our lives by His grace through our faith.

Scripture records several examples of people who experienced spectacular results because they praised God before there was any visible reason to do so. Let's examine two of these incidents—one involving the Apostle Paul and the other King Jehoshaphat.

PAUL AND SILAS:
DELIVERED THROUGH PRAISE

Paul and his co-worker, Silas, were proclaiming the good news of salvation through faith in Christ in the Macedonian city of Philippi. When they encountered a slave girl possessed with a devil, Paul set her free by commanding the evil spirit to leave. The girl's owners were furious because they made money off of her demon-inspired ability to tell fortunes. The men complained to city authorities who, in turn, arrested Paul and Silas, beat them and put them in stocks in the dungeon of the Philippian prison. The Bible records that: *"At midnight Paul and Silas prayed, and sang praises to God: and the prisoners heard them"* (Acts 16:25).

Suddenly there was a great earthquake. The prison doors flew open and everyone's bonds were loosed. The occurrence so moved the keeper of the prison that he begged Paul and Silas to tell him what he must do to be saved from his sin. Paul did so and the man, his family, and his entire household acknowledged Jesus as Savior and Lord. Tradition tells us that this jailer became the pastor of a church established in Philippi.

Note what happened here. Paul and Silas were preaching—doing the work of the Lord—when they set a girl free from bondage to Satan. For this godly act, they were repaid with a severe beating and imprisonment. Yet, they made a choice to rejoice by praising God. Why? Because they felt like it? That's highly unlikely. They praised God because they knew from the scripture that it is always appropriate to praise the Lord.

"I will bless the Lord at all times: his praise shall continually be in my mouth" (Psalm 34:1).

"Oh that men would praise the Lord for his goodness, and for his wonderful works to the children of men" (Psalm 107:15).

"From the rising of the sun unto the going down of the same the Lord's name is to be praised" (Psalm 113:3).

"At midnight I will rise to give thanks unto thee because of thy righteous judgments" (Psalm 119:62).

What was the result of their praise? God received honor and Paul and Silas prepared a path for Him to demonstrate His salvation to them. Genuine bad—unjust imprisonment—became genuine good. The apostle and his co-laborer were released from jail and the overseer of the prison became overseer of a church.

JEHOSHAPHAT AND JUDAH: VICTORIOUS THROUGH PRAISE

Three enemy armies came against Jehoshaphat, king of Judah, the southern kingdom of Israel. Jehoshaphat and his people were greatly outnumbered. They didn't know what to do, so they sought God's help. God spoke to them through His prophet and promised to help. The next day, as they prepared for battle, Jehoshaphat exhorted his people to believe what God had told them and to stand firm.

"After consulting the leaders of the people, the king appointed singers to walk ahead of the army, singing to the Lord and praising him for his holy splendor. This is what they sang: 'Give thanks to the Lord; his faithful love endures forever'" (2 Chronicles 20:21, NLT).

Did these people feel like praising God? Probably not. Based on what they could see, they were doomed—about to be overwhelmed by a much larger force. Surely they felt the same fear we feel when we face a formidable enemy. However, they chose to rejoice and their response brought them deliverance.

"At the moment they began to sing and give praise, the Lord caused the armies of Ammon, Moab, and Mount Seir to start fighting among themselves. ...So when the army of Judah arrived at the lookout point in the wilderness, there were dead bodies lying on the ground for as far as they could see. Not a single one of the enemy had escaped" (2 Chronicles 20:22-24, NLT).

Observe what happened in this incident. Jehoshaphat and Judah were hopelessly outmanned, yet they believed God's promise to help them. As they went into battle, they expressed their faith by sending men ahead of the army to proclaim God's goodness and wonderful works. What was the result? Judah won a marvelous victory that day. Their powerful triumph came through praise, not military might. Scripture says, *"For the Lord had made them to rejoice over their enemies"* (2 Chronicles 20:27). They beat their enemies with praise.

Praise prepared the way for God to show them His salvation. Praise stopped the enemy and stilled the avenger. And God was glorified as the fear and awe of the Lord came on the surrounding kingdoms when they heard what He had done for Israel.

THE CURE FOR COMPLAINING

Not only does praise glorify God and open the door to His power, it is a cure for the destructive habit of complaining. Complaining expresses discontent. It is the opposite of gratefulness. When we encounter life's trials, many of us talk about what we don't have and what isn't going right. Then we turn to God with a long list of complaints about our situation and a "help me please" tacked onto the end of our prayer. But when we complain, we aren't speaking Heaven's language. Thankfulness is the only language spoken in Heaven.

Complaining actually brings further trouble. Remember the Israelites on the way from Egypt to Canaan? They grumbled about the many challenges they encountered and brought destruction on themselves (Numbers 21:4-6). The Bible warns us not to make the same mistake. "(Don't) *discontentedly complain as some of them did and were put out of the way entirely by the destroyer [death]"* (1 Corinthians 10:10, AMP).

Praise to God is the antidote for complaining. There is always something to be grateful for in every situation, including the good we can see and the good we do not yet see. Despite the challenges the children of Israel faced as they traveled the difficult route to Canaan, they had much to be thankful for throughout their journey. They could have praised God for their mighty deliverance from Egyptian slavery. They could have thanked God for the wonderful land to which He was leading them. They could have rejoiced over the food, water, guidance and protection God gave as they navigated through the desert wilderness. But instead, they complained.

You and I also have much to be thankful for no matter what we are facing. We can praise God that He has delivered us from the kingdom of darkness and made us His son or daughter through faith in Christ. We can thank Him that we have a beautiful home awaiting us in Heaven. We can rejoice that God is with us and for us and that He will get us through until He gets us out, just like He did Israel.

WHAT AND WHY

What should we do when tribulation comes our way? We should count it all joy or consider it as an occasion to respond with praise and thanksgiving to God. Why should we do it?

- It is always appropriate to praise the Lord no matter what is happening in our lives.

- Praise glorifies and honors God.

- Praise stops the enemy and stills the avenger.

- Praise prepares the way for God to show us His salvation.

In the face of adversity, we can boldly proclaim the goodness of God and His wonderful works to the children of men. We can be grateful for what God has already done, is doing and will do. In every situation, instead of complaining, we can make a choice to rejoice.

If you don't have the right perspective on life's trials, it can be hard to thank and praise the Lord when troubles come. We will address this issue in the next chapter.

THE RIGHT PERSPECTIVE ON TROUBLES

*I*t is vital that we learn to view life's troubles from the standpoint of eternity. An eternal perspective makes it easier to rejoice no matter what happens. Compared to forever, even a lifetime of suffering is miniscule. Nobody in Heaven is crying about anything they encountered during their time on earth. I'm not minimizing the very real pain and suffering people experience. I am simply putting hardships into perspective to help lighten the load of life's adversities.

In this chapter, we want to consider the perspectives of Paul, Joseph and Moses. Despite the many challenges they faced, their perspective helped them praise God. And each man witnessed God work mightily in their circumstances as He brought good out of bad.

PAUL'S PERSPECTIVE

The Apostle Paul saw his life from the standpoint of eternity, which made it possible for him to rejoice, even in prison. He wrote the following words:

*"For our light and momentary troubles are achieving
for us an eternal glory that far outweighs them all.
So we fix our eyes not on what is seen, but on what
is unseen. For what is seen is temporary, but what is
unseen is eternal"* (2 Corinthians 4:17-18, NIV).

Paul's viewpoint enabled him to call the many hardships, persecutions and afflictions he endured "momentary" and "light." This doesn't mean Paul liked or enjoyed them. It means his troubles didn't weigh him down because they were small in comparison to eternity. Paul realized that his life on earth was a very tiny part of his existence and that his troubles would not last forever. This vantage point helped him keep the pains of life in perspective.

Notice that Paul said he focused his attention on what he could not see instead of his circumstances. He did this by remembering words from scripture about the goodness and works of God. Paul knew that the unseen kingdom of God, with its full power and provision, would outlast, and ultimately change, what he could see. Therefore, he based his view of life on this greater reality.

Paul is now in Heaven enjoying the blessings of endless life with the Lord. He has long forgotten the years he spent in prison, the beatings he endured and the shipwrecks he suffered. Such a day is coming for you and me—a day when what we are currently experiencing will not matter at all. The joys awaiting us will banish the hurts of life. Viewing our misfortunes in the light of eternity helps us praise God no matter what we see and feel.

Paul also was aware that the sufferings he experienced as he preached the gospel were producing eternal results.

Multitudes came to faith in Christ through his ministry. This awareness helped him keep a right perspective on his troubles. The sufferings were worth the effort because of the outcome. This knowledge helped Paul rejoice in extremely challenging circumstances.

You may think that Paul's life had eternal consequences because he was a great apostle, but your life could never match up to his. God doesn't expect you to replicate Paul's life. He expects you to live the life you've been given. The Bible is filled with examples of ordinary people who carried out the mundane and the difficult tasks of life. All the while, God worked behind the scenes to produce everlasting results. Consider one example.

Jonathan's Arrow Carrier

After David killed Goliath in their famous battle, King Saul had David come live in his home. But Saul, who was increasingly jealous of David's success and growing popularity, became intent on killing him. David fled for his life. Saul's son, Jonathan, found David and told him he was sure his father meant him no harm. The two men came up with a strategy to find out the king's true intentions. Jonathan planned to discuss the situation with Saul and report his findings to David.

David faced potential danger from Saul, so he and Jonathan decided to unveil Saul's intentions in an unusual way. At a prearranged time, Jonathan would go out to a nearby field where David was hiding and shoot some arrows. If Jonathan shot the arrows one way, it meant Saul was not a threat to David. If the arrows went to another spot, it meant David needed to flee.

Jonathan discerned that Saul intended to kill David, so he sent his arrows in the direction that conveyed this message. Notice the point that is relevant to our study. Jonathan took his young servant with him to pick up the arrows.

> *"'Start running,'* (Jonathan) *told the boy, 'so that you can find the arrows as I shoot them.' So the boy ran and Jonathan shot an arrow beyond him. When the boy had almost reached the arrow, Jonathan shouted, 'The arrow is still ahead of you. Hurry, hurry, don't wait.' So the boy quickly gathered up the arrows and ran back to his master.* **He, of course, didn't understand what Jonathan meant; only Jonathan and David knew.** *Then Jonathan gave his bow and arrows to the boy and told him to take them back to the city"* (1 Samuel 20:36-40, TLB).

What a seemingly valueless task—running around on a hot day picking up arrows shot by a rich prince. The arrow carrier had no idea that the arrows he retrieved sent a critical message to David or that he was part of an event with eternal consequences. The information he unknowingly communicated helped preserve David's life so that he could become king of Israel, father Solomon, and continue the family line through which Jesus the Savior would eventually come.

I am certain that when you and I get to Heaven, we will encounter people whose eternal destiny was affected by their interaction with us in the ordinary affairs of life. Just like Jonathan's arrow carrier, our daily activities may seem meaningless and mundane. However, if we realized that God is at work behind the scenes as He gathers His family, it would lighten the load and lessen the pressure of our circumstances.

This perspective will help us rejoice—despite what we see—just as it helped Paul.

JOSEPH'S PERSPECTIVE

Like Paul, Joseph responded with praise to God throughout the many challenges he encountered. When Joseph arrived in Egypt as a slave, Potiphar purchased him and soon noticed that God caused Joseph to prosper. When Joseph went to prison for rape, the prison keeper also noted that God helped Joseph (Genesis 39:1-4; 21-23).

These two men could not see God with their eyes, but they knew that God aided Joseph. How? Joseph must have acknowledged God in a demonstrable way. To acknowledge God means to praise Him by talking about who He is and what He has done, is doing and will do. Clearly, Joseph praised God in the presence of Potiphar and the jailer.

Take My Bones Back

Joseph also had an eternal perspective. He recognized that there is more to life than just this life. That knowledge helped him deal with the many adversities he faced.

God made two promises to Joseph before his trials began. God promised him greatness and He pledged to give him a homeland in Canaan (Genesis 37:5-8; Genesis 35:9-12). God fulfilled the call to greatness in Joseph's lifetime, but Joseph never returned home to live. He died in Egypt. Shortly before his death, Joseph told his family to carry his bones to Canaan when they returned to their country, as he knew they would one day.

" 'Soon I will die,' Joseph told his brothers, 'but God will surely come for you, to lead you out of this land of Egypt. He will bring you back to the land he vowed to give the descendants of Abraham, Isaac, and Jacob.' Then Joseph made the sons of Israel swear an oath, and he said, 'When God comes to lead us back to Canaan, you must take my body back with you.' So Joseph died at the age of 110. They embalmed him, and his body was placed in a coffin in Egypt" (Genesis 50:24-26, NLT).

Four hundred years later, when Joseph's family finally left Egypt, they took his bones with them as he had instructed. Moses saw to it.

"The Israelites left Egypt like a marching army. Moses took the bones of Joseph with him, for Joseph had made the sons of Israel swear that they would take his bones with them when God led them out of Egypt—as he was sure God would" (Exodus 13:18-19, NLT).

Joseph realized that his destiny did not end when he died. He knew there was coming a day when he would again live in the land of his birth. Joseph is in Heaven right now awaiting his return to earth with Jesus at His Second Coming. At that time, Joseph's bones will be raised up and restored to life and he will be reunited with his body at the resurrection of the dead. The first place his feet will stand is Canaan, which will fulfill God's second promise to Joseph.

We can find relief from the stress and pain of unfulfilled dreams when we are aware that there is more to life than just this life. All will be made right in the life to come. This perspective helps lighten the load and makes it easier for us to praise God in the midst of our trials. It did so for Joseph and will do the same for us.

MOSES' PERSPECTIVE

There is no doubt that Moses was a man of praise. After passing through the Red Sea, he and the rest of Israel sang the praises of the Only All-Powerful God.

> *"I will sing to the Lord, for he has triumphed gloriously; he has thrown both horse and rider into the sea. The Lord is my strength and my song; he has become my victory. He is my God, and I will praise him; he is my father's God, and I will exalt him"* (Exodus 15:1-2, NLT).

Moses didn't just rejoice *after* he saw God deliver them. He proclaimed God's goodness *before* he witnessed it. The Bible says that Moses acknowledged God at the edge of the Promised Land in the face of walled cities and giants. Moses declared God's past help, present provision and future promises. In other words, he praised God.

> *"But I said to* (the people of Israel), *'Don't be afraid! The Lord your God is going before you. He will fight for you, just as you saw him do in Egypt. And you saw how the Lord your God cared for you again and again here in the wilderness, just as a father cares for his child. Now he has brought you to this place'"* (Deuteronomy 1:29-31, NLT).

Moses also composed several songs recorded in scripture, including Psalm 91 and the Song of Moses (Deuteronomy 32). They give us insight into Moses' view of life. Moses understood the importance of declaring who God is and what He does despite how things look. Moses wrote:

> *"He that dwelleth in the secret place of the most High shall abide under the shadow of the Almighty.* **I will say** *of the Lord, He is my refuge and my fortress: my God; in him will I trust"* (Psalm 91:1-2).

> *"***I will proclaim** *the name of the Lord; how glorious is our God! He is the Rock; his work is perfect. Everything he does is just and fair. He is a faithful God who does no wrong; how just and upright he is"* (Deuteronomy 32:3-4, NLT).

Not only was Moses a man of praise, he was a man who lived with eternity in view. Moses grew up as a prince of Egypt. But when he came of age, he turned down the privilege and power of his position and chose to suffer with the Hebrew people. Moses realized that the pleasures of life in Pharaoh's court were short-lived, but the hardships he endured for the sake of service to Christ would win him never-ending benefits.

> *"By faith Moses, when he had grown up, refused to be known as the son of Pharaoh's daughter. He chose to be mistreated along with the people of God rather than to enjoy the pleasures of sin for a short time. He regarded disgrace for the sake of Christ as of greater value than the treasures of Egypt, because he was looking ahead to his reward"* (Hebrews 11:24-26, NIV).

Moses found the strength to reject the riches and authority of Egypt by looking past what he could see in his surroundings to the Invisible God and His kingdom.

*"By faith he left Egypt, not fearing the king's anger;
he persevered because he saw him who is invisible"*
(Hebrews 11:27, NIV).

Moses understood that the sufferings and losses of this life are minor compared to the joys and recompense ahead. Like Paul and Joseph, he looked beyond what he could see to Almighty God, who was with him and for him. Moses' perspective made it possible for him to praise God no matter what came his way.

· →→→▶ · ◀◀◀← ·

There is more to life than this present moment. There is more to life than just this life. When you learn to see life's troubles in terms of forever, it lightens the load. When you view your hardships from the standpoint of eternity, it's easier to thank and praise the Lord. This, in turn, prepares the way for Him to show you His salvation, both in this life and in the life to come.

RESPOND, DON'T REACT

*I*f we are going to deal with life's challenges in a way that brings glory to God and good to us, we have to learn to *respond* rather than *react* to the hardships of life. You might think, "What's the difference?"

Suppose you walk down a hallway and I leap out from behind a door and shout "Boo!" You would most likely react by jumping back as you let out a scream. In that moment, my little surprise would direct your behavior. When you react to something, that event dictates your actions.

A response is different. To respond means "to answer." When you respond to an incident, you answer it with the Word of God. You begin to talk about who God is and what He has done, is doing and will do. The situation does not drive your behavior. God's Word directs your actions as you praise God by acknowledging Him.

WHAT DIFFERENCE DOES IT MAKE?

Reacting and responding also produce different results. Let's look at some examples of the consequences of responding versus reacting.

Jacob's Reaction

We examined Joseph's story in Chapter 7. It is a spectacular account of how God worked to bring great good out of challenging circumstances. We learned that Joseph was a man who *responded* to his ordeal by acknowledging God. We noted that his ability to respond helped him deal effectively with his trials. However, in Joseph's story, we also find a man who *reacted* to trouble—Jacob, Joseph's father.

Jacob lost his favorite son, Joseph, when his other sons sold Joseph into slavery. Many years later, during a great famine, Jacob sent the surviving sons (except for Benjamin, the youngest) down to Egypt to buy provisions. Once in Egypt, the brothers appeared before the man in charge of food distribution. It was Joseph. He recognized his siblings, but they did not recognize him. Joseph gave them the supplies they requested but put the men through a series of tests to see if their characters had changed since he last saw them. In one of those tests, Joseph demanded that they bring Benjamin to him. Joseph planned to hold another brother, Simeon, in an Egyptian prison until they followed his orders and brought Benjamin to him.

Jacob's sons returned to Canaan with plenty of food, but without Simeon. They told their father what happened and Jacob *reacted* to their report. He let the circumstances dictate his behavior.

96

*"Jacob exclaimed, 'You have deprived me of my children! Joseph has disappeared, Simeon is gone, and now you want to take Benjamin, too. **Everything is going against me!**'"* (Genesis 42:36, NLT).

Jacob's reaction was completely appropriate based on what he could see. Everything seemed to be going wrong. But sight doesn't have all the facts in any situation—including this one. In reality, God was at work behind the scenes. Everything was not against Jacob. The events that took place were actually leading to tremendous blessings for Jacob and his family. Jacob would not lose Benjamin or Simeon. He was about to be reunited with his long-lost son Joseph. And he and his family would receive a place to live in Egypt that included a full supply of food that would last the rest of the years of famine.

What effect did Jacob's reaction have? Although it did not halt God's plan to reconnect him with Joseph and Simeon or move the family to Egypt, Jacob's pronouncement of doom added to his own emotional pain. His reactive words made a difficult predicament more stressful for everyone.

What should Jacob have done? He could have *responded* to his sons' account of the trip to Egypt by recalling God's past help and proclaiming His promise of present and future provision. Such a response would have given Jacob and his family hope and lessened the anguish produced by the events in Egypt.

Israel's Reaction

Earlier, we referenced Israel at the border of Canaan. You may recall that twelve spies were sent in to scout out the country. They returned to the awaiting Israelites with a dire report of walled cities and enemies that were too big to conquer.

"We can't go up against them! They are stronger than we are! ...The land we explored will swallow up any who go to live there. All the people we saw were huge. ...We felt like grasshoppers next to them, and that's what we looked like to them" (Numbers 13:31-33, NLT).

Israel *reacted* by letting the spies' report about the land determine their actions. They ultimately refused to enter Canaan. In this case, reacting did more than bring the Hebrews additional emotional duress. It also cost them God's will. That entire generation (with the exception of two men) never possessed the land that God intended for them.

Two of the spies *responded* rather than reacted to what they discovered on their scouting mission. Joshua and Caleb saw the same obstacles the other ten spies observed, yet they assessed their circumstances in terms of what God said. They responded to the opposition in the land with God's promise to fight for them.

" 'Let's go at once to take the land,' (Caleb) said. 'We can certainly conquer it' " (Numbers 13:30, NLT).

"(Joshua said) Do not rebel against the Lord, and don't be afraid of the people of the land. They are only helpless prey to us! They have no protection, but the Lord is with us! Don't be afraid of them" (Numbers 14:9, NLT).

Joshua and Caleb's response emboldened them to enter Canaan, conquer their enemies, and take possession of all that God had promised them. We should heed these examples from scripture and develop our ability to respond rather than react.

HOW DO WE RESPOND?

We noted in Chapter 9 that the Bible instructs us to view trials as opportunities to rejoice (James 1:2). That is another way of saying *respond to tribulation*. However, it is impossible to do so without accurate knowledge from the Bible. That's why we've taken time to cover the various issues outlined in this book.

We've considered a number of accounts in scripture that show us how God works in the midst of life's challenges and what He is able to accomplish. We've looked at cases where God used human choice and its consequences—even those He did not condone—and caused them to serve His purposes. We've seen instances where God took real evil and brought genuine good out of it. Those narratives were recorded to help us.

"Such things were written in the Scriptures long ago to teach us. They give us hope and encouragement as we wait patiently for God's promises" (Romans 15:4, NLT).

With the information we've gleaned from the Bible, we now know how to respond. When troubles come your way, acknowledge God. Talk about who God is and what He has done, is doing and will do. Recall the times that God has helped you in the past and remember His promise of present and future provision. Instead of proclaiming what you see and feel, answer your trials by declaring what God says about your difficulty.

• This situation is not bigger than God and it did not take Him by surprise. He already has a plan in mind to deal with it. I'm going to praise and thank Him for His help before I see it.

- God is working behind the scenes in this circumstance to bring maximum glory to Himself and maximum good to me and as many people as possible.

- God will cause all this to serve His purposes as He brings genuine good out of genuine bad.

- My Heavenly Father does things at the right time and at the proper time, I'll see results. If short-term blessing has to be put off for long-term eternal good, that's alright with me. I trust Him to do what's best in this case.

- God will get me through until He gets me out. He can cause me to thrive in the midst of this trial.

When you respond in this manner, you are proclaiming the way things really are according to God instead of how they look. Then, like Joshua and Caleb, you'll find the courage to act in agreement with God.

Responding to a situation doesn't mean you deny the trouble. Instead, you look past it with the help of the Bible. God's Word assures you that there is more to the situation than what you see and feel. His Word reveals that God is with you and His Presence is the help you need. No matter how daunting the trial looks, remember that it is temporary and subject to change by God's power.

"God is our refuge and strength...a very present and well-proved help in trouble" (Psalm 46:1, AMP).

"Hope in God, for I shall again praise Him for the help of His presence" (Psalm 42:5, NASB).

YET, I WILL REJOICE

When you face catastrophic circumstances, you have to make the choice to rejoice. This can be difficult when everything you see and feel says "fall apart" and "give up." But it is worth the effort to respond rather than react.

The prophet Habakkuk faced this kind of predicament. He ministered in Israel's southern kingdom, Judah, in the final days of its national existence. Due to repeated unrepentant idol worship, the nation was about to be crushed by the Babylonian Empire, Jerusalem burned to the ground, and the people exiled to a foreign land. Scripture records Habakkuk's response to the coming calamity.

> *"Even though the fig trees have no blossoms, and there are no grapes on the vine; even though the olive crop fails, and the fields lie empty and barren; even though the flocks die in the fields, and the cattle barns are empty,* ***yet I will rejoice*** *in the Lord!* ***I will be joyful*** *in the God of my salvation. The Sovereign Lord is my strength! He will make me as surefooted as a deer and bring me safely over the mountains"* (Habakkuk 3:17-19, NLT).

Notice that Habakkuk says nothing about feeling joyful. He spoke of exercising his will and making a choice to respond appropriately in the situation. How could he do that? He knew that his circumstances weren't bigger than the Sovereign Lord. He was assured that God would be his strength and would bring him safely through whatever was ahead. This knowledge lightened the load and prepared the way for God to show Habakkuk His salvation.

With accurate knowledge from the Bible about who God is and how He works in our lives, we can truly praise the Lord for His goodness and His wonderful works to the children of men. No matter what we see around us, we can acknowledge the Invisible God and His help, confident that at the right time we will see tangible results. When we learn to respond to life's challenges by answering them with God's Word, we can overcome in even the most difficult trials.

CONCLUSION

There's no such thing as a trouble-free life in this fallen world. All of us encounter challenges ranging from minor annoyances to major calamities. There is no way to avoid life's adversities, so we must have answers to the two big questions: *Why did this happen? What is God doing?* The purpose of this book has been to address these *why* and *what* questions. I trust you now know how to answer them according to what the Bible says.

- Why are troubles here? They are part of life in a sin cursed earth, a world that has been negatively affected by sin beginning with Adam in the Garden of Eden.

- What is God doing? Although God is never the source of life's trials, He is able to cause them to serve His purposes and to bring great good out of genuine evil as He gathers His family for eternity.

We've examined a number of accounts in the Bible of *real* people who faced *real* problems and received *real* help from God. These examples show us how God uses the trials of life for His glory and for the good of His people. Hopefully, you've drawn encouragement from their stories.

We have also discussed the *why* and *what* questions in regard to ourselves.

- What should we do when troubles come our way? Make a choice to rejoice. Acknowledge God. Consider it an occasion to praise the Lord by talking about who He is and what He has done, is doing and will do.

- Why should we rejoice? Because it's always appropriate to praise the Lord for His goodness and wonderful works to the children of men.

Whatever life brings your way, you can face it with the assurance that your trials did not come from God. You can be certain that your adversities did not take Him by surprise. God knew about your situation before He formed the earth and He has a plan in mind to deal with it. No matter what the trial, it's not bigger than God. He will get you through until He gets you out. Therefore, you can answer your challenge with His Word and glorify God as you prepare the way for Him to show you His salvation.

When this current ordeal is behind you, you will be able to look back and see clearly that God kept His Word. He brought maximum glory to Himself and maximum good to as many people as possible—including you—as He worked out His plan for a family.